GREAT
FOLK TALES
OF
IRELAND

Great
Folk Tales
of
Ireland

Compiled and introduced
by
Mary McGarry

Illustrations by
Richard Hook

FREDERICK MULLER LIMITED
LONDON

First published in Great Britain in 1972
by Wolfe Publishing Limited.

This edition published 1979 by Frederick Muller Limited
London, NW2 6LE.

Second impression 1980

British Library Cataloguing in Publication Data

McGarry, Mary
    Great folk tales of Ireland.
    1. Tales, Irish
    I. Title
    398.2'1'09415   GR153.5

    ISBN 0–584–62330–5

Printed and bound in Great Britain by
Billing & Sons Limited, Guildford, London and Worcester

Contents

Note : For the names of the characters, the spelling used is that of the original story. The spelling therefore sometimes varies from story to story.

Introduction

Story-telling has always been an intrinsic part of the Celtic way of life, an amusement as old as the race itself. The narratives, peopled with both deities and mortals who dwell in a land of adventure, warfare and romance, form perhaps one of the oldest vernacular literatures of any European nation. The Celtic realm is a veritable treasure trove for the keen folklorist, and indeed for all who enjoy an exciting fireside tale.

The monastic scribe of the late Middle Ages preserved much of this heritage of lore in the ornate, vellum manuscripts of "The Book of Leinster" or "The Book of the Dun Cow". But it is the strong oral tradition of the Irish people which has enabled a living folklore to survive. Over the centuries story-telling was an esteemed profession. Poets, bards and "seanachai" (Gaelic story-tellers) who enjoyed the privileged patronage of the Irish chiefs, were an essential part of any festive gathering, where they recited poems and tales for the entertainment of the guests. The influence of alien cultures and the expansion of modern life has unfortunately led to the decline of this class, and the number of "seanachai" today is rapidly dwindling. Luckily the wealth of their memories will be saved for future generations in the archives of the Irish Folklore Commission, which since 1935 has systematically collected and annotated these native sources.

Peig Sayers (1873–1958) is perhaps the best known of this "dying race"; a native of the Blasket Islands off the Dingle peninsula, she could in her time recount no fewer than three hundred and seventy-five narratives. To find the real culture of modern Ireland one must look to her folklore, for here in stories handed down from age to age are endless clues to the great mythological epics of the past.

The shades of prehistory can be lifted by a study of some of the folk tradition, because scholarship has established a reasonable

7

historical basis for several well-known tales. But whether factual or fictitious, the accounts give free rein to the fertile Celtic imagination. The Ulster and Fenian cycles are possibly in character the most spectacular section of Irish legends and are certainly the most popular. The events of the Ulster cycle revolve around the ancient kingdom of the same name and are approximately dated to the first century before Christ. Cuchulainn, the central hero, plays an important role in the victory of the North over Maeve, Queen of Connaught. The inclusion of an excerpt from the boyhood deeds of this warrior gives an idea of his stature in Irish folklore.

In "The Book of Leinster" lies the most famous single story of the Ulster cycle, "The story of Deirdre", a source of inspiration for Yeats, Synge and others. The narrative, which relates the tragic fate of Deirdre and her lover Naois at the hands of Deirdre's betrothed, Connachar, King of Ulster, shows many similarities to the story of Tristan and Iseult, and the other great romance of the Fenian cycle, that of Diarmuid and Grainne. It is also known as one of "The Three Sorrowful Tales of Erin", along with "The Fate of the Children of Lir". The legend of the transformation by magic of Lir's family into wild swans has its counterparts in other popular European mythologies.

The Fenian cycle, traditionally assigned to the third century A.D., depicts the adventures of the band of warriors known as the "Fianna". Their leader, Finn MacCumhail, is just one of a host of heroic figures portrayed for Irish children. Oisin, Finn's son, is the subject of both prose and poetry, which describe his journey to the land of eternal youth, "Tir na nOg". The rigorous requirements for entry into the "Fianna" illustrate the fact that it was no mean feat to be included in its membership, and might make it comparable to the legendary Arthur and his "Knights of the Round Table".

Irish folklore is not restricted to the heroic but covers a wide range of traditions. The hauntings of the "Pooka" mingle with tales of fairy changelings, or the imaginative origin of the Lough of Cork, as told in Crofton Croker's "Fior Usga". Samuel Lover relates anecdotes collected on a visit to Clonmacnoise in "The King and the Bishop" which, if slightly stage-Irish in character, nevertheless shows the vitality of Irish local tradition and humour.

In any collection such as this one feels that merely the tip of the iceberg is being touched; only a taste provided to arouse one's interest. However, I hope that this introduction to what Yeats aptly termed "The Celtic Twilight" may encourage the reader to delve more deeply into a world, the limits of which still lie in the hazy Irish mist.

Mary McGarry
Dublin, May 1972

The Fate of the Children of Lir

BY JOSEPH JACOBS

t happened that a long time ago in the age of gods and heroes, the Sea God, Lir, married a foster-daughter of Bodb the Red, King of the gods. She bore him four children; a daughter called Fionula, then a son called Aed and two others, twin boys, called Fiachra and Conn. But at the birth of the twins she died and Lir was left sorrowing.

After some time Lir visited the court of his father-in-law and married the sister of his dead wife, whom he thought would be a good mother to his children. For a time all went well. The princess, called Aeife, treated her stepchildren kindly. But then Aeife began to be jealous of the tenderness and attention shown by Lir to Fionula and her brothers, and to fear he loved them better than he did her. At last the wish for their death came into her heart and she began to plot to destroy them.

First she tried to bribe the servants to murder them, but this failed. Fearing to kill them herself, she led them away to a lonely lake, where she sent them into the water to bathe. Then from under her cloak she drew out a wand, such as the Druids used, and making an incantation over the children she turned them all into swans.

But although she had enough magical power to change their shapes, she could not take from them their speech or human hearts.

Fionula, the lovely girl who was now a swan, swam into the reeds just below the bank where Aeife was standing, and rearing her proud head she said: "Wicked and treacherous woman, give us back our human shapes, or Lir our father will punish you."

But Aeife smiled scornfully. "The lake is deep, and the children of Lir were drowned," she said. "That is the story I shall tell their father."

No words of beseeching would change the wicked Aeife's heart, or make her withdraw the spell.

Fionula spoke once more. "How long must we remain swans?" she asked bravely.

"Better if you had not asked me," replied Aeife. "But I will tell you. Three hundred years shall you remain upon this lake; and three hundred years upon the Sea of Moyle, the sea which lies between Erin and Alba; and three hundred years more beside the Isle of Glora in Erris."

"If you had killed us," cried Aed, "it had been kinder!"

"Nay," replied Aeife, "for after this moment you shall not remember your grief at being swans. But your human speech and human hearts, these shall you keep and you shall be able to sing more sweetly and more softly than swans have ever yet sung. Fare you well. I could have loved you had not your father loved you too dearly."

And with one wild gesture, half triumphant, half tragic, Aeife turned her back upon the lake and upon the four swans. But as she mounted the hill that lay between the lake and her palace she heard the swans singing, singing so sweetly and so softly that for a moment she paused to listen and then, plunging her fingers into her ears, she hurried on.

When Aeife got home she found Lir waiting for her. "You have been gone long," he said, "you and the children."

Aeife began to weep and wail of how the children had been disobedient and how they had drowned in the strong current and reeds in the lake.

But Lir in great grief cried out: "This is not true! You who pretended to love my children with a mother's love, you have led them away, you have led them away!" Here he was able to say no more, but rushed away from Aeife and ran towards the lake.

The lake lay shimmering like silver under the beams of the summer moon. And as he stood there, four swans came sailing towards him, their wings widened as if to enfold him. And one, the one who had been his daughter, began to speak in the tones he loved so well. She told him all the tragic story, and Conn, the youngest of the twins, broke in, begging his father to restore their human shape.

"I want to run and play with my brother," he said. "Just as we used to run and play before magic touched us."

Then Lir wrung his hands in agony. "Would that I had power enough," he said sorrowfully. "But I am, after all, such a puny god, I who had thought I ruled the sea."

"Do not grieve, my lord," said Fionula very gently. "We are not so unhappy. We love you and remember you are our father. If you will come down every night at sunset, then we will talk to you; then we will sing to you, and you will forget."

But anger against the false woman Aeife arose again in the heart of the Sea God. He caressed the heads of the swans, and his tears fell fast as he turned to leave them, and even their song which followed him up the hillside could not soothe his rage.

He went to Bodb the Red, who asked for proof of the evil deed. Lir led him to the lake, where the swans floated in the red light of the dawn. And they told their own tale, without passion or anger, until the end came and the toll of their sentence—three hundred years upon the Lake of Darvra, three hundred years upon the Sea of Moyle, three hundred years beside the Isle of Glora.

Lir asked Bodb to use his magic to bring back his children. But Bodb the Red turned to him a face of pain and pity and said sadly that his magic too was not enough to restore them to their father.

Yet Bodb the Red could punish Aeife. She came before the King quietly, as one in deep sorrow. She had put away her jewels, and over her golden hair she wore the veil of mourning.

The King began to tell her the story of the swans, while Aeife boldly pretended that the children had been claimed by the waters of the lake.

The King twirled his Druid's wand and said: "I shall not ask you, Aeife, what has become of the children of Lir. I shall not ask you what you can do to restore them to their sorrowing father. He stands there, you can look at him and see how stricken he is. You can listen, Aeife, for the soft voice of Fionula, and look long for the lithe form of young Aed to stride over the fairy hills. You can run fleet of foot across the green grass, but never again will Conn or Fiachra overtake you, or their gay young laughter gladden your heart. But my question is far away from talk of the lost children of Lir. Answer me truly, Aeife, what do you fear more than my wand?"

Aeife, in great terror at the wand waving above her head, was compelled to answer: "To be a demon, a demon of the air, with no rest for body or soul."

She shrieked wildly, and she tried to clutch the wand, but it swept over her like the sword of an avenger, and her human shape fell from her like a beautiful dress. Then she rose as if she had wings, the wings of a vampire or a great bat, and again she shrieked, like a shrill wind before a storm, and flew far away. Over the hills she went, and over the Lake of Darvra. The sky was black with clouds, and from the distant mountains came the heavy roll of thunder. No heart, no speech, no song had the King of the gods left her—only her wickedness, and a demon's shape to carry her about for ever like a bird of ill omen.

All the gods of the Gaels came to hear of the sweet singing of the swans and went down to the Lake of Darvra to listen to it. It became a custom amongst gods and mortals to hold a yearly feast in honour of the swans.

But at the end of three hundred years the second part of the spell began. The swans had to leave the beautiful lake they knew so well, and fly away to the cold north to make their home upon the bleak and stormy Sea of Moyle.

Upon the Sea of Moyle, far away from gods and men, the four swans suffered the worst of weather. In lonely exile they spent day and night buffeted by wind and storm, haunted by the cries of ship-wrecked mariners and terrified by the monsters of the deep. Forbidden to land, their feathers in the bitter winters froze against the sharp rocks, and only their love for each other remained of the happy past.

During this sad time Fionula, the eldest of the four, became as a mother to the rest, wrapping her plumage round the youngest ones when the frost left a white rime on the rocks. With Conn on her right hand always, and Fiachra on her left, she kept Aed in front of her. "For," she said, "so I can shelter you all with my wings."

At last they entered on the third stage of their ordeal and went to the wild Isle of Glora; and there, too, they suffered loneliness and fear. The years rolled by. On the shores of Erris they first heard the sound of a church bell, which filled them with wonder.

As the time of their sentence drew to an end, they wished to return to the palace of their father Lir. Soon the air was filled with the sound of wings in strong flight, as the four swans winged their way towards Ireland. But when they came to look for their old home, all they could see was a few great mounds, clumps of nettles and windswept bushes. The palace was there, but from their eyes it was hidden, because they were destined for higher things than a return to the land of their youth.

With great sadness they flew slowly back to Erris, and then again they heard the thin sound of a bell. Terrified, the swans listened. The bell stopped and from a tiny chapel a man dressed in the robe of a hermit came out and made his way down towards them on the shore. The old hermit heard their story and the four swans made their home beside the little chapel and every day said over the simple prayers that he taught them. Their sorrow lightened; their beautiful song was heard again.

Now it happened that a Princess of Munster was to wed a powerful chief, and begged from him as a bridal token the four wonderful swans that sung so well. The chief tried to bribe the hermit to part with the swans with gifts of bronze and silver for the chapel.

But the old man waved him away saying: "There is no price for a human soul. Under their plumage beat human hearts. Enchantment is still heavy upon them, but God is merciful, and their penance draws nigh to its end."

However, the chief seized hold of the silver chains which coupled the swans and dragged them away. But when the swans were ordered to sing before the bride, not a note could they utter. Then the face of the princess froze stiff in horror, for from the four swans fell away their snowy plumage and before her cowered an aged woman and three withered old men. Nine hundred years had passed over their heads and the days of gods and heroes had gone for ever. The bride ran shrieking from the palace.

But the hermit, seeing that the Angel of Death would soon claim them, sprinkled each meek white head with the water of holiness, and to each gave promise of life everlasting.

Fionula stretched out her arms towards the other three, and asked that they be laid in one grave, with Conn placed on her right hand and Fiachra on her left, and Aed before her face where she could see him. So that with her wings she could shelter them, as she had done upon the stormy Sea of Moyle.

Thus did the hermit lay the four children of Lir to rest at last.

Fior Usga

BY T. CROFTON CROKER

a little way beyond the Gallows Green of Cork, and just outside the town, there is a great lough of water, where people in the winter go and skate for the sake of diversion. But the sport above the water is nothing to what is under it, because at the very bottom of this lough there are buildings and gardens far more beautiful than any now to be seen. And how they came there was in this manner.

Long before Saxon foot pressed Irish ground there was a great King, called Corc, whose palace stood where the lough is now, in a round green valley that was just a mile about. In the middle of the courtyard was a spring of fair water, so pure and so clear that it was the wonder of all the world. Much did the King rejoice at having so great a curiosity within his palace, but as people came in crowds from far and near to draw the precious water of this spring, he was sorely afraid that in time it might become dry.

So he caused a high wall to be built up around it, and would allow nobody to have the water, which was a very great loss to the poor people living about the palace. Whenever he wanted any for himself he would send his daughter to get it, not liking to trust his servants with the key of the well-door, fearing they might give some of the water away.

One night the King gave a grand entertainment, and there were many great princes present, and lords and nobles without end. There were wonderful doings throughout the palace: there were bonfires, whose blaze reached up to the very sky; and dancing was there, to such sweet music that it ought to have waked up the dead out of their graves; and feasting was there in the greatest of plenty for all who came; nor was anyone turned away from the palace gates, but "you're welcome—you're welcome heartily," was the porter's salute for all.

Now it happened at this grand entertainment there was one young prince above all the rest mighty comely to behold, and as tall and as straight as ever eye would wish to look on. Right merrily did he dance that night with the old King's daughter, wheeling there, as light as a feather, and footing it away to the admiration of everyone. The musicians played the better for seeing their dancing; and they danced as if their lives depended upon it.

After all this dancing came the supper, and the young prince was seated at table by the side of his beautiful partner, who smiled upon him as often as he wished, for he had constantly to turn to the company and thank them for the many compliments passed upon his fair partner and himself.

In the midst of this banquet one of the great lords said to King Corc, "May it please your majesty, here is everything in abundance that heart can wish for, both to eat and drink, except water."

"Water!" said the King, mightily pleased at someone calling for that of which purposely there was a want. "Water shall you have, my lord, speedily, and that of such a delicious kind that I challenge all the world to equal it. Daughter," said he, "go and fetch some in the golden vessel which I caused to be made for the purpose."

The King's daughter, who was called Fior Usga (which signifies "Spring Water" in English), did not much like to be told to perform so menial a service before so many people; and though she did not venture to refuse the commands of her father, yet she hesitated to obey him, and looked down upon the ground.

The King, who loved his daughter very much, seeing this was sorry for what he had desired her to do, but having said the word he was never known to recall it. He therefore thought of a way to make his daughter go speedily to fetch the water, and this was by proposing that the young prince, her partner, should go along with her.

Accordingly, in a loud voice, he said, "Daughter, I wonder not at your fearing to go alone so late at night; but I doubt not the young prince at your side will go with you."

The prince was not displeased at hearing this and, taking the golden vessel in one hand, with the other he led the King's daughter out of the hall so gracefully that all present gazed after them with delight.

When they came to the spring of water, in the courtyard of the palace, the fair Usga unlocked the door with the greatest care. But

stooping down with the golden vessel to take some of the water out of the well, she found the vessel so heavy that she lost her balance and fell in. The young prince tried to save her, but in vain, because the water rose and rose so fast that the entire courtyard was speedily covered with it, and he hastened back almost in a state of distraction to the King.

The door of the well being left open the water, so long confined, rejoiced at obtaining its liberty and rushed forth incessantly, every moment rising higher; it reached the hall of the entertainment sooner than the young prince himself, so that when he attempted to speak to the King he was up to his neck in water. At length the water rose to such a height that it filled the entire green valley in which the King's palace stood, and so the present Lough of Cork was formed.

Yet the King and his guests were not drowned, as would now happen if such an inundation were to take place. Neither was his daughter, the fair Usga, who returned to the banquet hall the very next night after this dreadful event. And every night since then the same entertainment and dancing goes on in the palace in the bottom of the lough, and it will last until someone has the luck to bring up out of it the golden vessel which was the cause of all the mischief.

Nobody can doubt that it was a judgment upon the King for his shutting up the well in the courtyard from the poor people. And if there are any who do not credit my story, they might go and see the Lough of Cork, for there it is to be seen to this day. The road to Kinsale passes at one side of it and when its waters are low and clear the tops of towers and stately buildings may be plainly viewed in the bottom by those who have good eyesight, without the help of spectacles.

The White Trout: A Legend of Cong

BY SAMUEL LOVER

here was wanst upon a time, long ago, a beautiful lady who lived in a castle upon the lake beyant, and they say she was promised to a King's son, and they wor to be married, when all of a sudden he was murthered, the crathur (Lord help us), and threwn into the lake above, and so, of course, he couldn't keep his promise to the fair lady—and more's the pity.

Well, the story goes that she went out iv her mind, bekase av loosin' the King's son—for she was tendher-hearted, God help her, like the rest iv us!—and pined away after him, until at last, no one about seen her, good or bad; and the story wint that the fairies took her away.

Well, sir, in coorse o' time, the White Throut, God bless it, was seen in the sthrame beyant, and sure the people didn't know what to think av the crathur, seein' as how a white throut was never heard av afor, nor since. For years upon years the throut was there, just where you seen it this blessed minit, longer nor I can tell—aye throth, and beyant the memory o' th' ouldest in the village.

At last the people began to think it must be a fairy—for what else could it be? And no hurt nor harm was iver put an the white throut, until some wicked sinners of sojers kem to these parts, and laughed at all the people, and gibed and jeered them for thinkin' o' the likes. One o' them in partic'lar (bad luck to him; God forgi' me for saying it!) swore he'd catch the throut and ate it for his dinner—the blackguard.

Well, what would you think o' the villainy of the sojer? Sure enough he cotch the throut, and away wid him home, and puts

21

an the fryin'-pan, and into it he pitches the purty little thing. The throut squeeled all as one as a christian crathur, and, my dear, you'd think the sojer id split his sides laughin'—for he was a harden'd villain. When he thought one side was done, he turns it over to fry the other, and, what would you think, but the devil a taste of a burn was an it at all. Sure the sojer thought it was a quare throut that could not be briled. "But," says he, "I'll give it another turn by-and-by," little thinkin' what was in store for him, the haythen.

Well, when he thought that side was done he turns it agin, and lo and behold you, the divil a taste more done that side was nor the other. "Bad luck to me," says the sojer, "but that bates the world," says he. "But I'll thry you agin, my darlint," says he, "as cunnin' as you think yourself."

And so with that he turns it over and over, but not a sign of the fire was on the purty throut. "Well," says he, "my jolly little throut, maybe you're fried enough, though you don't seem over-well dress'd; but you may be better than you look, like a singed cat, and a tit-bit afther all," says he.

With that he ups with his knife and fork to taste a piece o' the throut. But, my jew'l, the minit he puts his knife into the fish, there was a murtherin' screech, that you'd think the life id lave you if you hurd it. Away jumps the throut out av the fryin'-pan into the middle o' the flure and an the spot where it fell, up riz a lovely lady—the beautifullest crathur that eyes ever seen, dressed in white, and a band o' gold in her hair, and a sthrame o' blood runnin' down her arm.

"Look where you cut me, you villain," says she, and she held out her arm to him—and, my dear, he thought the sight id lave his eyes.

"Couldn't you lave me cool and comfortable in the river where you snared me, and not disturb me in my duty?" says she.

Well, he thrimbled like a dog in a wet sack, and at last he stammered out somethin', and begged for his life, and ax'd her lady-ship's pardon, and said he didn't know she was on duty, or he was too good a sojer not to know bether nor to meddle wid her.

"I was on duty, then," says she. "I was watchin' for my true love that is comin' by wather to me," says the lady, "an' if he comes while I'm away, an' that I miss iv him, I'll turn you into a pinkeen, and I'll hunt you up and down for ever more, while the grass grows or wather runs."

Well, the sojer thought the life id lave him, at the thoughts iv his bein' turned into a pinkeen, and begged for mercy.

And with that says the lady: "Renounce your evil coorses," says she, "you villain, or you'll repint it too late. Be a good man for the futher and go to your duty reg'lar. And now," says she, "take me back and put me into the river again, where you found me."

"Oh, my lady," says the sojer, "how could I have the heart to drownd a beautiful lady like you?"

But before he could say another word, the lady was vanished, and there he saw the little throut an the ground. Well, he put it in a clean plate, and away he runs for the bare life, for fear her lover would come while she was away. And he run, and he run, even till he came to the cave agin, and threw the throut into the river. The minit he did, the wather was as red as blood for a little while, by rayson av the cut, I suppose, until the sthrame washed the stain away; and to this day there's a little red mark an the throut's side, where it was cut.

Well, sir, from that day out the sojer was an altered man, and reformed his ways, and went to his duty reg'lar, and fasted three times a-week—though it was never fish he tuk an fastin' days, for afther the fright he got, fish id never rest an his stomach—savin' your presence.

But anyhow, he was an altered man, as I said before, and in coorse o' time he left the army, and turned hermit at last. They say he used to pray evermore for the soul of the White Throut.

The Boyhood of Cuchulainn

TRANSLATED BY
STANDISH HAYES O'GRADY

his boy," said Fergus, "was reared in his father's and mother's house, by the seaside northwards in the plain of Muirthemne, where someone gave him an account of the macrad or 'boy-corps' of Emain Macha; how that Conchobar divides his day into three parts:

"the first being devoted to watching the boy-corps at their sport, especially that of hurling;

"the second to the playing of chess and draughts;

"the third to pleasurable consuming of meat and drink until drowsiness sets in, which then is promoted by the exertions of minstrels and musicians to induce favourable placidity of mind and disposition.

"And, for all that we are banished from him," continued Fergus, "by my word I swear that neither in Ireland nor in Scotland is there a warrior his (i.e., Conchobar's) counterpart.

"The little lad, then, as aforesaid, having heard of all this, one day told his mother that he was bent on a visit to Emain Macha to test the boy-corps at their own sports. She objected that he was immature, and ought to wait until some grown warrior or other, or some confidential of Conchobar's should, in order to insure his safety, bind over the boy-corps to keep the peace toward him. He told his mother that that was too long an outlook, that he could not wait, and that all she had to do was to set him a course for Emain Macha, since he did not know in which direction it lay.

" 'It is a weary way from here,' said the mother, 'for between thee and it lies Sliab Fuait.'

" 'Give me the bearings,' said he; and she did so.

"Away he went then, taking with him his hurly of brass, his ball of silver, his throwing javelin, and his toy spear, with which equipment he fell to shortening the way for himself. He did it thus: with his hurly he would strike the ball and drive it a great distance; then he pelted the hurly after it, and drove it just as far again; then he threw his javelin, lastly the spear. Which done, he would make a playful rush after them all, pick up the hurly, the ball and the javelin, while, before the spear's tip could touch the earth, he had caught the missile by the other end.

"In due course Cuchulainn reached Emain Macha, where he found the boy-corps, thrice fifty in number, hurling on the green and practising martial exercises with Conchobar's son, Fallomain, at their head. The lad dived right in among them and took a hand in the game. He got the ball between his legs and held it there, not suffering it to travel higher up than his knees or lower down than his ankle-joints, and so making it impossible for them to get in a stroke or in any other way to touch it.

"In utter amazement the whole corps looked on, but Follamain mac Conchobar cried: 'Good now, boys, all together meet this youngster as he deserves, and kill him; because it is taboo to have such a one join himself to you and interfere in your game, without first having had the civility to procure your guarantee that his life should be respected. Together then and at once attack him and avenge violation of your taboo; for we know that he is the son of some petty Ulster warrior, such as without safe-conduct is not accustomed to intrude into your play.'

"The whole of them assailed Cuchulainn, and simultaneously sent their hurlies at his head. He, however, parried all the hundred and fifty and was unharmed. The same with the balls, which he fended off with fists, fore-arms, and palms alone. Their thrice fifty toy spears he received in his little shield, and still was unhurt. In turn now, Cuchulainn went among them, and laid low fifty of the best. Five more of them," said Fergus, "came past the spot where myself and Conchobar sat at chess-play, with the young lad close in their wake.

" 'Hold, my little fellow,' said Conchobar, 'I see this is no gentle game thou playest with the boy-corps.'

" 'And good cause I have too,' cried Cuchulainn. 'After coming out of a far land to them, I have not had a guest's reception.'

" 'How now, little one,' said the King, 'knowest thou not the boy-corps conditions? That a newcomer must have them bounded by their honour to respect his life?'

" 'I knew it not,' said the boy, 'otherwise I had conformed, and taken measures beforehand.'

" ' 'Tis well,' said the king, 'take it now upon yourselves to let the boy go safe.'

" 'We do,' the boy-corps answered.

" 'They resumed play. Cuchulainn did as he would with them, and again laid out fifty of them on the ground. Their fathers deemed they could not but be dead. No such thing, however; it was merely that with his blows and pushes and repeated charges, he so terrified them that they took to the grass.

" 'What on earth is he at with them now?' asked Conchobar.

" 'I swear by my gods,' said Cuchulainn, 'that until they in their turn come under my protection and guarantee, I will not lighten my hand from off them.'

"This they did at once. Now," said Fergus in conclusion. "I submit that a youngster who did all this when he was just five years old needs not to excite our wonder, because, now being turned of seventeen years, he in this Cattle-Raid of Cooley cut a four-pronged pole and the rest, and that he should have killed a man, or two, or three men, or even—as indeed he has done—four."

9th CENTURY

The Kildare Pooka

BY PATRICK KENNEDY

r. H————R————, when he was alive, used to live a good deal in Dublin, and he was once a great while out of the country on account of the "ninety-eight" business. But the servants kept on in the big house at Rath———— all the same as if the family was at home. Well, they used to be frightened out of their lives after going to their beds, with the banging of the kitchen door, and the clattering of fire-irons, and the pots and plates and dishes.

One evening they sat up ever so long, keeping one another in heart with telling stories about ghosts and fetches, and that when—what would you have of it?—the little scullery boy, who used to be sleeping over the horses, and could not get room at the fire, crept into the hot hearth, and when he got tired listening to the stories, sorra fear him, but he fell dead asleep.

Well and good, after they were all gone and the kitchen fire raked up, the boy was woke with the noise of the kitchen door opening, and the trampling of an ass on the kitchen floor. He peeped out, and what should he see but a big ass, sure enough, sitting on his curabingo and yawning before the fire. After a little the ass looked about him, and began scratching his ears as if he was quite tired, and says he, "I may as well begin first as last."

The poor boy's teeth began to chatter in his head, for says he, "Now he's goin' to ate me."

But the fellow with long ears and tail on him had something else to do. He stirred the fire, and then he brought in a pail of water from the pump and filled a big pot that he put on the fire before he went out. He then put his hand—foot, I mean—into the hot hearth, and pulled out the little boy, who let a roar out of him with the fright. But the pooka only looked at him, and thrust out his lower lip to show how little he valued him, and then he pitched him into his pew again.

Well, the Pooka then lay down before the fire till he heard the boil coming on the water, and maybe there wasn't a plate, or a dish, or a spoon on the dresser that he didn't fetch and put into the pot, and wash and dry the whole bilin' of 'em as well as e'er a kitchen-maid from that to Dublin town. He put all of them up in their places on the shelves; and if he didn't give a good sweepin' to the kitchen, leave it till again.

Then he comes and sits fornent the boy, let down one of his ears, and cocked up the other, and gave a grin. The poor fellow strove to roar out, but not a dheeg 'ud come out of his throat. The last thing the pooka done was to rake up the fire, and walk out, giving such a slap o' the door, that the boy thought the house couldn't help tumbling down.

Well, to be sure if there wasn't a hullabaloo next morning when the poor fellow told his story! They could talk of nothing else the whole day. One said one thing, another said another, but a fat, lazy scullery girl said the wittiest thing of all. "Musha!" says she, "If the pooka does be cleaning up everything that way when we are asleep, what should we be slaving ourselves for doing his work?"

"Shu gu dheine," says another, "them's the wisest words you ever said, Kauth. It's meeself won't contradict you." So said, so done. Not a bit of a plate or dish saw a drop of water that evening, and not a besom was laid on the floor and everyone went to bed soon after sundown.

Next morning everything was as fine as fine in the kitchen, and the lord mayor might eat his dinner off the flags. It was great ease to the lazy servants, you may depend, and everything went on well till a fool-hardy gag of a boy said he would stay up one night and have a chat with the pooka.

He was a little daunted when the door was thrown open and the ass marched up to the fire.

"And then, sir," says he, at last, picking up courage, "if it isn't taking a liberty, might I ax who you are, and why you are so kind as to do half of the day's work for the girls every night?"

"No liberty at all," says the pooka, says he. "I'll tell you, and welcome. I was a servant in the time of Squire R———'s father, and was the laziest rogue that ever was clothed and fed, and done nothing for it. When my time came for the other world, this is the punishment was laid on me—to come here and do all this labour every night, and then go out in the cold. It isn't so bad in the fine weather: but if you only knew what it is to stand with

your head between your legs, facing the storm, from midnight to sunrise, on a bleak winter night."

"And could we do anything for your comfort, my poor fellow?" says the boy.

"Musha, I don't know," says the pooka. "But I think a good quilted frieze coat would help to keep the life in me them cold long nights."

"Why then, in troth, we'd be the ungratefullest of people if we didn't feel for you."

To make a long story short, the next night but two the boy was there again and if he didn't delight the poor pooka, holding up a fine warm coat before him, it's no mather! Betune the pooka and the man, his legs was got into the four arms of it, and it was buttoned down the breast and the belly, and he was so pleased he walked up to the glass to see how he looked.

"Well," says he, "it's a long lane that has no turning. I am much obliged to you and your fellow-servants. You have made me happy at last. Goodnight to you."

So he was walking out, but the other cried: "Och, sure you're going too soon! What about the washing and sweeping?"

"Ah, you may tell the girls that they must now get their turn. My punishment was to last till I was thought worthy of a reward for the way I'd done my duty. You'll see me no more."

And no more they did, and right sorry they were for having been in such a hurry to reward the ungrateful pooka.

How Cormac MacArt went to Faery

BY JOSEPH JACOBS

ormac, son of Art, son of Conn of the Hundred Battles, was High King of Ireland, and held his Court at Tara. One day he saw a youth upon the green having in his hand a glittering faery branch with nine apples of red. And whensoever the branch was shaken, wounded men and women enfeebled by illness would be lulled to sleep by the sound of the very sweet faery music which those apples uttered; nor could anyone upon earth bear in mind any want, woe or weariness of soul when the branch was shaken for him.

"Is that branch thy own?" said Cormac.

"It is indeed mine."

"Wouldst thou sell it? And what wouldst thou require for it?"

"Will you give me what I ask?" said the youth.

The King promised, and the youth then claimed his wife, his daughter and his son. Sorrowful of heart was the King, heaviness of heart filled his wife and children when they learned that they must part from him. But Cormac shook the branch amongst them, and when they heard the soft, sweet music of the branch they forgot all care and sorrow and went forth to meet the youth, and he and they took their departure and were seen no more.

Loud cries of weeping and mourning were made throughout Erin when this was known, but Cormac shook the branch so that there was no longer any grief or heaviness of heart upon anyone.

After a year Cormac said: "It is a year today since my wife, my son, and my daughter were taken from me. I will follow them by the same path that they took."

Cormac went off, and a dark magical mist rose about him, and he chanced to come upon a wonderful, marvellous plain. Many

C   33

horsemen were there, busy thatching a house with the feathers of foreign birds. When one side was thatched they would go and seek more, and when they returned, not a feather was on the roof. Cormac gazed at them for a while and then went forward.

Again, he saw a youth dragging up trees to make a fire, but before he could find a second tree the first one would be burnt, and it seemed to Cormac that his labour would never end.

Cormac journeyed onwards until he saw three immense wells on the border of the plain, and on each well was a head. From out of the mouth of the first head there flowed two streams, into it there flowed one. The second head had a stream flowing out of and another stream into its mouth, whilst three streams were flowing from the mouth of the third head.

Great wonder seized Cormac, and he said: "I will stay and gaze upon these wells, for I should find no man to tell me their story."

With that he set onwards till he came to a house in the middle of a field. He entered and greeted the inmates. There sat within a tall couple clad in many-hued garments, and they greeted the King, and bade him welcome for the night.

Then the wife bade her husband seek food, and he arose and returned with a huge wild boar upon his back and a log in his hand. He cast down the swine and the log upon the floor, and said: "There is meat; cook it yourselves."

"How can I do that?" said Cormac.

"I will teach you," said the man. "Split this great log, make four pieces of it, and make four quarters of the hog. Put a log under each quarter, tell a true story, and the meat will be cooked."

"Tell the first story yourself," said Cormac.

"Seven pigs I have of the same kind as the one I bought, and I could feed the world with them. For if a pig is killed I have but to put its bones into the sty again, and it will be found alive the next morning."

The story was true, and a quarter of the pig was cooked.

Then Cormac begged the woman of the house to tell a story.

"I have seven white cows, and they fill seven cauldrons with milk every day, and I give my word that they yield as much milk as would satisfy the men of the whole world if they were out on yonder plain drinking it."

The story was true, and a second quarter of the pig was cooked.

Cormac was bidden now to tell a story for his quarter, and he told how he was upon a search for his wife, his son and his

34

daughter that had been borne away from him a year before by a youth with a faery branch.

"If what thou sayest be true," said the man of the house, "thou art indeed Cormac, son of Art, son of Conn of the Hundred Battles."

"Truly I am," quoth Cormac.

That story was true, and a quarter of the pig was cooked.

"Eat thy meal now," said the man of the house.

"I never ate before," said Cormac, "having only two people in my company."

"Wouldst thou eat it with three others?"

"If they were dear to me, I would," said Cormac.

The door opened, and there entered the wife and children of Cormac. Great was his joy and his exultation.

Then Manannan mac Lir, lord of the faery cavalcade, appeared before him in his own true form, and said thus: "I it was, Cormac, who bore away these three from thee. I it was who gave thee this branch, all that I might bring thee here. Eat now and drink."

"I would do so," said Cormac, "could I learn the meaning of the wonders I saw today."

"Thou shalt learn them," said Manannan. "The horsemen thatching the roof with feathers are a likeness of people who go forth into the world to seek riches and fortune. When they return their houses are bare, and so they go on for ever.

"The young man dragging up the trees to make a fire is a likeness of those who labour for others: much trouble they have, but they never warm themselves at the fire.

"The three heads in the wells are three kinds of men. Some there are who give freely when they get freely; some who give freely though they get little; some who get much and give little—and they are the worst of the three, Cormac," said Manannan.

After that Cormac and his wife and his children sat down, and a tablecloth was spread before them.

"That is a very precious thing before thee," said Manannan. "There is no food however delicate that shall be asked of it but it shall be had without doubt."

"That is well," quoth Cormac.

After that Manannan thrust his hand into his girdle and brought out a goblet and set it upon his palm.

"This cup has this virtue," said he, "that when a false story is told before it, it makes four pieces of it, and when a true story is related it is made whole again."

"Those are very precious things you have, Manannan," said the King.

"They shall all be thine," said Manannan. "The goblet, the branch and the tablecloth."

Then they ate their meal, and that meal was good, for they had only to think of any meat and they got it upon the tablecloth, and any drink, which they got in the cup. Great thanks did they give to Manannan.

When they had eaten their meal, a couch was prepared for them and they laid down to slumber and sweet sleep. Where they rose on the morrow morn was in Tara of the Kings, and by their side were tablecloth, cup and branch.

Thus did Cormac fare at the Court of Manannan, and this is how he got the faery branch.

The Brewery of Egg-shells

BY T. CROFTON CROKER

t might be considered impertinent were I to explain what is meant by a changeling. Both Shakespeare and Spenser have already done so, and who is there unacquainted with *A Midsummer Night's Dream* and *The Faerie Queene*?

Now Mrs. Sullivan fancied that her youngest child had been exchanged by "fairies' theft", and certainly appearances warranted such a conclusion; for in one night her healthy, blue-eyed boy had become shrivelled up into almost nothing, and never ceased squalling and crying. This naturally made poor Mrs. Sullivan very unhappy and all the neighbours, by way of comforting her, said that her own child was, beyond any kind of doubt, with the good people, and that one of themselves was put in his place.

Mrs. Sullivan of course could not disbelieve what everyone told her, but she did not wish to hurt the thing. For although its face was so withered, and its body wasted away to a mere skeleton, it had still a strong resemblance of her own boy. She therefore could not find it in her heart to roast it alive on the griddle, or to burn its nose off with the red-hot tongs, or to throw it out in the snow on the roadside—notwithstanding these, and several like proceedings, were strongly recommended to her for the recovery of her child.

One day who should Mrs. Sullivan meet but a cunning woman, well known about the country by the name of Ellen Leah (or Grey Ellen). She had a gift, however she got it, of telling where the dead were, and what was good for the rest of their souls. She could charm away warts and wens, and do a great many wonderful things of the same nature.

"You're in grief this morning, Mrs. Sullivan," were the first words of Ellen Leah to her.

"You may say that, Ellen," said Mrs. Sullivan, "and good cause I have to be in grief. For there was my own fine child whipped off from me out of his cradle, without as much as 'by your leave' or 'ask your pardon,' and an ugly dony [tiny] bit of a shrivelled-up fairy put in his place. No wonder then that you see me in grief, Ellen."

"Small blame to you, Mrs. Sullivan," said Ellen Leah. "But are you sure 'tis a fairy?"

"Sure?" echoed Mrs. Sullivan. "Sure enough I am to my sorrow, and can I doubt my own two eyes? Every mother's soul must feel for me!"

"Will you take an old woman's advice?" said Ellen Leah, fixing her wild and mysterious gaze upon the unhappy mother. After a pause, she added, "but maybe you'll call it foolish?"

"Can you get me back my child, my own child, Ellen?" said Mrs. Sullivan with great energy.

"If you do as I bid you," returned Ellen Leah, "you'll know." Mrs. Sullivan was silent in expectation, and Ellen continued: "Put down a big pot, full of water, on the fire, and make it boil like mad; then get a dozen new-laid eggs, break them, and keep the shells, but throw away the rest; when that is done, put the shells in the pot of boiling water, and you will soon know whether it is your own boy or a fairy. If you find that it is a fairy in the cradle, take the red-hot poker and cram it down his ugly throat, and you will not have much trouble with him after that, I promise you."

Home went Mrs. Sullivan, and did as Ellen Leah desired. She put the pot on the fire, and plenty of turf under it, and set the water boiling at such a pace, that if ever water was red-hot, it surely was.

The child was lying, for a wonder, quite easy and quiet in the cradle, every now and then cocking his eye, that would twinkle as keen as a star in a frosty night, over at the great fire, and the big pot upon it. And he looked on with great attention at Mrs. Sullivan breaking the eggs and putting down the egg-shells to boil. At last he asked, with the voice of a very old man, "What are you doing, Mammy?"

Mrs. Sullivan's heart, as she said herself, was up in her mouth ready to choke her, at hearing the child speak. But she contrived to put the poker in the fire, and to answer without making any wonder at the words, "I'm brewing, a vick [my son]."

"And what are you brewing, Mammy?" said the little imp, whose supernatural gift of speech now proved beyond question that he was a fairy substitute.

"I wish the poker was red," thought Mrs. Sullivan; but it was a large one, and took a long time heating. So she determined to keep him in talk until the poker was in a proper state to thrust down his throat, and therefore repeated the question.

"Is it what I'm brewing, a vick," said she, "you want to know?"

"Yes, Mammy. What are you brewing?" returned the fairy.

"Egg-shells, a vick," said Mrs. Sullivan.

"Oh!" shrieked the imp, starting up in the cradle and clapping his hands together. "I'm fifteen hundred years in the world, and I never saw a brewery of egg-shells before!"

The poker was by this time quite red and Mrs. Sullivan, seizing it, ran furiously towards the cradle. But somehow or other her foot slipped, and she fell flat on the floor, and the poker flew out of her hand to the other end of the house.

However, she got up without much loss of time and went to the cradle, intending to pitch the wicked thing that was in it into the pot of boiling water. But there she saw her own child in a sweet sleep, one of his soft round arms rested upon the pillow; his features were as placid as if their repose had never been disturbed, save the rosy mouth, which moved with a gentle and regular breathing.

Who can tell the feelings of a mother when she looks upon her sleeping child? Why should I therefore endeavour to describe those of Mrs. Sullivan at again beholding her long-lost boy? The fountains of her heart overflowed with the excess of joy, and she wept. Tears trickled silently down her cheek, nor did she strive to stop them—they were tears, not of sorrow, but of happiness.

The Story of Deirdre

BY JOSEPH JACOBS

*t*here was a man in Ireland once who was called Malcolm Harper. The man was a right good man, and he had a goodly share of this world's goods. He had a wife, but no family. What did Malcolm hear but that a soothsayer had come home to the place, and as the man was a right good man, he wished that the soothsayer might come near them. Whether it was that he was invited or that he came of himself, the soothsayer came to the house of Malcolm.

"Are you doing any soothsaying?" says Malcolm.

"Yes, I am doing a little. Are you in need of soothsaying?"

"Well, I do not mind taking soothsaying from you, if you have soothsaying for me, and you would be willing to do it."

"Well, I will do soothsaying for you. What kind of soothsaying do you want?"

"Well, the soothsaying I wanted was that you would tell me my lot or what will happen to me, if you can give me knowledge of it."

"Well, I am going out, and when I return, I will tell you."

And the soothsayer went forth out of the house and he was not long outside when he returned.

"Well," said the soothsayer, "I saw in my second sight that on account of a daughter of yours the greatest amount of blood shall be shed that has ever been shed in Erin since time and race began. And the three most famous heroes that ever were found will lose their heads on her account."

After a time a daughter was born to Malcolm, and because of the soothsaying he did not allow a living being to come to his house, only himself and the nurse, He asked this woman: "Will you yourself bring up the child to keep her in hiding far away,

43

where eye will not see a sight of her nor ear hear a word about her!"

The woman said she would, so Malcolm got three men, and he took them away to a large mountain, distant and far from reach, without the knowledge or notice of anyone. He caused there a hillock, round and green, to be dug out of the middle, and the hole thus made to be covered carefully over so that a little company could dwell there together. This was done.

Deirdre and her foster-mother dwelt in the bothy mid the hills without the knowledge or the suspicion of any living person about them and without anything occurring, until Deirdre was sixteen years of age. Deirdre grew like the white sapling, straight and trim as the rash on the moss. She was the creature of fairest form, of loveliest aspect, and of gentlest nature that existed between earth and heaven in all Ireland; and whatever colour of hue she had before, there was nobody that looked into her face but she would blush fiery red over it.

The woman who had charge of her gave Deirdre every information and skill of which she herself had knowledge and skill. There was not a blade of grass growing from root, nor a bird singing in the wood, nor a star shining from heaven but Deirdre had a name for it. Yet one thing the woman did not wish her to have either part or parley with—any single living man of the rest of the world.

But on a gloomy winter night, with black, scowling clouds, a hunter of game was wearily travelling the hills, and what happened but that he missed the trail of the hunt, and lost his course and companions. A drowsiness came upon the man as he wearily wandered over the hills, faint from hunger and wandering, and benumbed with cold. When at last he lay down beside the green hill in which Deirdre lived, a deep sleep fell upon him and a troubled dream came to him. He thought that he enjoyed the warmth of a fairy broch, the fairies being inside playing music. The hunter shouted out in his dream, if there was anyone in the broch, to let him in for the Holy One's sake.

Deirdre heard the voice and said to her foster-mother: "O foster-mother, what cry is that?"

"It is nothing at all, Deirdre, merely the birds of the air astray and seeking each other. But let them go past to the bosky glade. There is no shelter or house for them here."

"Oh, foster-mother, the bird asked to get inside for the sake of God of the Elements, and you yourself tell me that anything

44

that is asked in His name we ought to do. If you will not allow the bird that is being benumbed with cold, and done to death with hunger, to be let in, I do not think much of your language or your faith. But since I give credence to your language and to your faith, which you taught me, I will myself let in the bird."

Deirdre arose and drew the bolt from the leaf of the door, and she let in the hunter. She placed a seat in the place for sitting, food in the place for eating, and drink in the place for drinking for the man who came to the house.

"Oh, for this life and raiment, you man that came in, keep restraint on your tongue!" said the old woman. "It is not a great thing for you to keep your mouth shut and your tongue quiet when you get a home and shelter of a hearth on a gloomy winter's night."

"Well," said the hunter, "I may do that—keep my mouth shut and my tongue quiet, since I came to the house and received hospitality from you. But by the hand of thy father and grand-father, and by your own two hands, if some other of the people of the world saw this beauteous creature you have here hid away, they would not long leave her with you, I swear."

"What men are these you refer to?" said Deirdre.

"Well, I will tell you, young woman," said the hunter. "They are Naois, son of Uisnech, and Allen and Arden his two brothers."

"What like are these men when seen, if we were to see them?" said Deirdre.

"Why, the aspect and form of the men when seen are these," said the hunter. "They have the colour of the raven on their hair, their skin like swan on the wave in whiteness, and their cheeks as the blood of the brindled red calf, and their speed and their leap are those of the salmon of the torrent and the deer of the grey mountainside. And Naois is head and shoulder over the rest of the people of Erin."

"However they are," said the nurse, "be you off from here and take another road. And, King of Light and Sun, in good sooth and certainty, little are my thanks for yourself or for her that let you in!"

The hunter went away, and went straight to the palace of King Connachar. He sent word in to the King that he wished to speak to him if he pleased. The King answered the message and came out to speak to the man. "What is the reason of your journey?" said the King to the hunter.

"I have only to tell you, O King," said the hunter, "that I saw the fairest creature that ever was born in Erin, and I came to tell you of it."

"Who is this beauty and where is she to be seen, when she was not seen before till you saw her, if you did see her?"

"Well, I did see her," said the hunter, "But, if I did, no man else can see her unless he gets directions from me as to where she is dwelling."

"And will you direct me to where she dwells? And the reward of your directing me will be as good as the reward of your message," said the King.

"Well, I will direct you, O King, although it is likely that this will not be what they want," said the hunter.

Connachar, King of Ulster, sent for his nearest kinsmen, and he told them of his intent. Though early rose the song of the birds mid the rocky caves and the music of the birds in the grove, earlier than that did Connachar, King of Ulster, arise, with his little troop of dear friends, in the delightful twilight of the fresh and gentle May. The dew was heavy on each bush and flower and stem, as they went to bring Deirdre forth from the green knoll where she stayed. Many a youth was there who had a lithe, leaping and lissom step when they started, whose step was faint, failing, and faltering when they reached the bothy on account of the length of the way and roughness of the road.

"Yonder now, down in the bottom of the glen, is the bothy where the woman dwells, but I will not go nearer than this to the old woman," said the hunter.

Connachar with his band of kinsfolk went down to the green knoll where Deirdre dwelt and he knocked at the door of the bothy. The nurse replied: "No less than a King's command and a King's army could put me out of my bothy tonight. And I should be obliged to you, were you to tell who it is that wants me to open my bothy door."

"It is I, Connachar, King of Ulster."

When the poor woman heard who was at the door, she rose with haste and let in the King and all that could get in of his retinue.

When the King saw the woman that was before him that he had been in quest of, he thought he never saw in the course of the day nor in the dream of night a creature so fair as Deirdre and he gave his full heart's weight of love to her. Deirdre was raised on the topmost of the heroes' shoulders and she and her foster-mother were brought to the Court of King Connachar of Ulster.

With the love that Connachar had for her, he wanted to marry Deirdre right off there and then, will she nill she marry him. But she said to him: "I would be obliged to you if you will give me the respite of a year and day."

He said: "I will grant you that, hard though it is, if you will give me your unfailing promise that you will marry me at the year's end." And she gave the promise.

Connachar got for her a woman-teacher and merry modest maidens fair that would lie down and rise with her, that would play and speak with her. Deirdre was clever in maidenly duties and wifely understanding, and Connachar thought he never saw with bodily eye a creature that pleased him more.

Deirdre and her women companions were one day out on the hillock behind the house enjoying the scene, and drinking in the sun's heat. What did they see coming but three men a-journeying? Deirdre was looking at the men that were coming, and wondering at them. When the men neared them, Deirdre remembered the language of the huntsman, and she said to herself that these were the three sons of Uisnech, and that this was Naois, he having what was above the bend of the two shoulders above the men of Erin all.

The three brothers went past without taking any notice of them, without even glancing at the young girls on the hillock. What happened but that love for Naois struck the heart of Deirdre, so that she could not but follow after him. She girded up her raiment and went after the men that went past the base of the knoll, leaving her women attendants there.

Allen and Arden had heard of the woman that Connachar, King of Ulster, had with him, and they thought that if Naois, their brother, saw her, he would have her himself, more especially as she was not married to the King. They perceived the woman coming, and called on one another to hasten their step as they had a long distance to travel, and the dusk of night was coming on. They did so.

She cried: "Naois, son of Uisnech, will you leave me?"

"What piercing, shrill cry is that—the most melodious my ear ever heard, and the shrillest that ever struck my heart of all the cries I ever heard?"

"Is it anything else but the wail of the wave-swans of Connachar?" said his brothers.

"No! Yonder is a woman's cry of distress," said Naois, and he swore he would not go farther until he saw from whom the cry came, and Naois turned back.

Naois and Deirdre met, and Deirdre kissed Naois three times, and a kiss each to his brothers. With the confusion that she was in, Deirdre went into a crimson blaze of fire, and her colour came and went as rapidly as the movement of the aspen by the stream side. Naois thought he never saw a fairer creature, and Naois gave Deirdre the love that he never gave to thing, to vision, or to creature but to herself. Then Naois placed Deirdre on the topmost height of his shoulder, and told his brothers to keep up their pace, and they kept up their pace.

Naois thought that it would not be well for him to remain in Erin on account of the way in which Connachar, King of Ulster, his kinsman, would go against him because of Deirdre, though he had not married her; and he turned back to Alba—that is, Scotland. He reached the side of Loch Ness and made his habitation there. He could kill the salmon of the torrent from out his own door, and the deer of the grey gorge out his window. Naois and Deirdre and Allen and Arden dwelt in a tower, and they were happy so long a time as they were there.

By this time the end of the period came when Deirdre had to marry Connachar, King of Ulster. Connachar made up his mind to take Deirdre away by the sword whether she was married to Naois or not. So he prepared a great and gleeful feast. He sent word far and wide through Erin all to his kinspeople to come to the feast. Connachar thought to himself that Naois would not come, though he should bid him; and the scheme that arose in his mind was to send for his father's brother, Ferchar Mac Ro, and to send him on an embassy to Naois.

He did so, and Connachar said to Ferchar: "Tell Naois, son of Uisnech, that I am setting forth a great and gleeful feast to my friends and kinspeople throughout the wide extent of Erin all, and that I shall not have rest by day nor sleep by night if he and Allen and Arden be not partakers of the feast."

Ferchar Mac Ro and his three sons went on their journey, and reached the tower where Naois was dwelling by the side of Loch Ness. The sons of Uisnech gave a cordial kindly welcome to Ferchar Mac Ro and his three sons, and asked of him the news of Erin.

"The best news that I have for you," said the hardy hero, "is that Connachar, King of Ulster, is setting forth a great sumptuous feast to his friends and kinspeople throughout the wide extent of Erin all, and he has vowed by the earth beneath him, by the high heaven above him, and by the sun that wends to the west, that he will have no rest by day nor sleep by night if the sons of Uisnech, the sons of his own father's brother, will not come back to the land of their home and the soil of their nativity, and to the feast likewise, and he has sent us on embassy to invite you."

"We will go with you," said Naois.

"We will," said his brothers.

But Deirdre did not wish to go with Ferchar Mac Ro, and she tried every prayer to turn Naois from going with him, She said: "I saw a vision, Naois, and do you interpret it to me." Then she sang:

> O Naois, son of Uisnech, hear
> What was shown in a dream to me.

> There came three white doves out of the South,
> Flying over the sea,
> And drops of honey were in their mouth
> From the hive of the honey-bee.

> O Naois, son of Uisnech, hear
> What was shown in a dream to me.

> I saw three grey hawks out of the south
> Come flying over the sea,
> And the red red drops they bare in their mouth
> They were dearer than life to me.

Said Naois:

> It is nought but the fear of woman's heart,
> And a dream of the night, Deirdre.

"The day that Connachar sent the invitation to his feast will be unlucky for us if we don't go, O Deirdre," said Naois.

"You will go there," said Ferchar Mac Ro. "And if Connachar show kindness to you, show ye kindness to him; and if he will display wrath towards you, display ye wrath towards him, and I and my three sons will be with you."

"We will," said Daring Drop.

"We will," said Hardy Holly.

"We will," said Fiallan the Fair.

"I have three sons, and they are three heroes, and in any harm or danger that may befall you, they will be with you, and I myself will be along with them." And Ferchar Mac Ro gave his vow and his word in presence of his arms that, if any harm or danger came in the way of the sons of Uisnech, he and his three sons would not leave head on live body in Erin, despite sword or helmet, spear or shield, blade or mail, be they ever so good.

Deirdre was unwilling to leave Alba, but she went with Naois. Deirdre wept tears in showers and she sang:

> Dear is the land, the land over there,
>   Alba full of woods and lakes;
> Bitter to my heart is leaving thee,
>   But I go away with Naois.

Ferchar Mac Ro did not stop till he got the sons of Uisnech away with him, despite the suspicion of Deirdre.

> The coracle was put to sea,
>   The sail was hoisted to it;
> And the second morrow they arrived
>   On the white shores of Erin.

As soon as the sons of Uisnech landed in Erin, Ferchar Mac Ro sent word to Connachar, King of Ulster, that the men whom he wanted were come, and let him now show kindness to them.

"Well," said Connachar, "I did not expect that the sons of Uisnech would come, though I sent for them, and I am not quite ready to receive them. But there is a house down yonder where I keep strangers, and let them go down to it today, and my house will be ready for them tomorrow."

But he that was up in the palace felt it long that he was not getting word as to how matters were going on for those down in the house of the strangers.

"Go you, Gelban Grednach, son of Lochlin's King, go you down and bring me information as to whether her former hue and complexion are on Deirdre. If they be, I will take her out with edge of blade and point of sword, and if not, let Naois, son of Uisnech, have her for himself," said Connacher.

Gelban, the cheering and charming son of Lochlin's King, went down to the place of the strangers, where the sons of Uisnech and Deirdre were staying. He looked in through the bicker-hole on the door-leaf. Now she that he gazed upon used to go into a crimson blaze of blushes when anyone looked at her. Naois looked at Deirdre and knew that someone was looking at her from the back of the door-leaf. He seized one of the dice on the table before him and fired it through the bicker-hole, and knocked the eye out of Gelban Grednach the Cheerful and Charming, right through the back of his head. Gelban returned back to the palace of King Connacher.

"You were cheerful, charming, going away, but you are cheerless, charmless, returning. What has happened to you, Gelban? But have you seen her, and are Deirdre's hue and complexion as before?" said Connachar.

"Well, I have seen Deirdre, and I saw her also truly, and while I was looking at her through the bicker-hole on the door, Naois, son of Uisnech, knocked out my eye with one of the dice in his hand. But of a truth and verity, although he put out even my eye, it were my desire still to remain looking at her with the other eye, were it not for the hurry you told me to be in," said Gelban.

Connachar ordered three hundred active heroes to go down to the abode of the strangers and to take Deirdre up with them and kill the rest.

"The pursuit is coming," said Deirdre.

"Yes, but I will myself go out and stop the pursuit," said Naois.

"It is not you, but we that will go," said Daring Drop, and Hardy Holly, and Fiallan the Fair. "It is to us that our father entrusted your defence from harm and danger when he himself left for home."

And the gallant youths, full noble, full manly, full handsome, with beauteous brown locks, went forth girt with battle arms fit for fierce fight and clothed for fierce contest with combat dress which was burnished bright, brilliant, bladed, blazing, on which were many pictures of beasts and birds and creeping things, lions and lithe-limbed tigers, brown eagle and harrying hawk and adder fierce; and the young heroes laid low three-thirds of the company.

Connachar came out in haste and cried with wrath: "Who is there on the floor of fight, slaughtering my men?"

51

"We, the three sons of Ferchar Mac Ro."

"Well," said the King, "I will give a free bridge to your grandfather, a free bridge to your father, and a free bridge each to you three brothers, if you come over to my side tonight."

"Well, Connachar, we will not accept that offer from you, nor thank you for it. Greater by far do we prefer to go home to our father and tell the deeds of heroism we have done, than accept anything on these terms from you. Naois, son of Uisnech, and Allen and Arden are as nearly related to yourself as they are to us, though you are so keen to shed their blood, and you shed our blood also, Connachar."

And the noble, manly, handsome youths with beauteous brown locks returned inside. "We are now," said they, "going home to tell our father that you are now safe from the hands of the King."

And the youths all fresh and tall and lithe and beautiful, went home to their father to tell that the sons of Uisnech were safe. This happened at the parting of the day and night in the morning twilight time.

And Naois said they must go away, leave that house, and return to Alba. So Naois and Deirdre, Allen and Arden started to return to Alba.

But word came to the King that the company he was in pursuit of were gone. The King then sent for Duanan Gacha Druid, the best magician he had, and he spoke to him as follows: "Too much wealth have I expended on you, Duanan Gacha Druid, to give schooling and learning and magic mystery to you, if these people get away from me today without care, without consideration or regard for me, without chance of overtaking them, and without power to stop them."

"Well, I will stop them," said the magician, "until the company you send in pursuit return." And the magician placed a wood before them through which no man could go, but the sons of Uisnech marched through the wood without halt or hesitation, and Deirdre held on to Naois's hand.

"What is the good of that? That will not do yet," said Connachar. "They are off without bending of their feet or stopping of their step, without heed or respect to me, and I am without power to keep up to them or opportunity to turn them back this night."

"I will try another plan on them," said the druid, and he placed before them a grey sea instead of a green plain. The three heroes stripped and tied their clothes behind their heads, and Naois placed Deirdre on the top of his shoulder.

They stretched their sides to the stream,
And sea and land were to them the same;
The rough grey ocean was the same
As meadow-land green and plain.

"Though that be good, O Duanan, it will not make the heroes
return," said Connachar. "They are gone without regard for me,
and without honour to me, and without power on my part to
pursue them or to force them to return this night."

"We shall try another method on them, since yon one did not
stop them," said the druid. And the druid froze the grey-ridged
sea into hardy rocky knobs, the sharpness of sword being on the
one edge and the poison power of adders on the other.

Then Arden cried that he was getting tired, and nearly giving
over. "Come you, Arden, and sit on my right shoulder," said
Naois. Arden came and sat on Naois's shoulder. Arden was long
in this posture when he died; but though he was dead Naois
would not let him go.

Allen then cried out that he was getting faint and nigh-well
giving up, and he gave forth the piercing sigh of death. But
Naois heard his cry and asked Allen to lay hold of him and he
would bring him to land.

Allen was not long when the weakness of death came on him
and his hold failed. Naois looked around, and when he saw his
two well-beloved brothers dead, he cared not whether he lived or
died, and he gave forth the bitter sigh of death, and his heart
burst.

"They are gone," said Duanan Gacha Druid to the King, "and
I have done what you desired me. The sons of Uisnech are dead
and they will trouble you no more; and you have your wife hale
and whole to yourself."

"Blessings for that upon you and may the good results accrue
to me, Duanan. I count it no loss what I spent in the schooling
and teaching of you. Now dry up the flood, and let me see if I
can behold Deirdre," said Connachar.

And Duanan Gacha Druid dried up the flood from the plain and
the three sons of Uisnech were lying together dead, without
breath of life, side by side on the green meadow plain and Deirdre
bending above showering down her tears.

Then Deirdre said this lament: "Fair one, loved one, flower of
beauty, beloved upright and strong, beloved noble and modest
warrior. Fair one, blue-eyed, beloved of thy wife, lovely to me

at the trysting-place came thy clear voice through the woods of Ireland. I cannot eat or smile henceforth. Break not today, my heart. Soon enough shall I lie within my grave. Strong are the waves of sorrow, but stronger is sorrow's self, Connachar."

The people then gathered round the heroes' bodies and asked Connachar what was to be done with the bodies. The order that he gave was that they should dig a pit and put the three brothers in it side by side.

Deirdre kept sitting on the brink of the grave, constantly asking the gravediggers to dig the pit wide and free. When the bodies of the brothers were put in the grave, Deirdre said:

> Come over hither, Naois, my love,
>   Let Arden close to Allen lie;
> If the dead had any sense to feel,
>   Ye would have made a place for Deirdre.

The men did as she told them. She jumped into the grave and lay down by Naois, and she was dead by his side.

The King ordered the body to be raised from out the grave and to be buried on the other side of the loch. It was done as the King bade, and the pit closed. Thereupon a fir shoot grew out of the grave of Deirdre and a fir shoot from the grave of Naois, and the two shoots united in a knot above the loch. The King ordered the shoots to be cut down, and this was done twice, until, at the third time, the wife whom the King had married caused him to stop this work of evil and his vengeance on the remains of the dead.

How the Shannon Acquired its Name

BY PATRICK KENNEDY

a long time ago there was a well in Ossory, shaded by a rowan tree. When the berries became ripe they would drop into the water, and be eaten by the salmon that had their residence in the well. Red spots would then appear on the fish, and they received the name of "Salmon of Knowledge". It was not so easy to take these salmon, for there were shelving banks, and they could also retreat into the cavern from which the waters issued that supplied the well.

However, one was occasionally caught, and the captor, as soon as he had made his repast on it, found himself gifted with extra-ordinary knowledge, even as Fion, son of Cumhail, when he had tasted of the broiled salmon of the Boyne.

It was understood that no woman could taste of this delicacy and live. Yet Sionan, a lady cursed with an extraordinary desire of knowledge, braved the danger, suspecting the report to be spread abroad and maintained by the male sex from merely selfish motives. So, in order to lose no time, she had a fire ready by the side of the well, and the unfortunate fish was scarcely flung out on the grass when he was frying on the coals.

Who can describe the rapture she felt from the burst of light that filled her mind on swallowing the first morsel! Alas—the next moment she was enveloped by the furious waters, which, bursting forth, swept westwards, and carried the unfortunate lady with them till they were lost in the great river which ever after bore her name.

The King and the Bishop

BY SAMUEL LOVER

Samuel Lover in his travels visits the ruined abbey of Clonmacnoise.

ne day I was accosted by a peasant who had watched for a long time, in silent wonder, the draft of the stone cross, as it grew into being beneath my pencil; and finding the man apt, as the ghost says to Hamlet, I entered into conversation with him. To some remark of mine touching the antiquity of the place, he assured me "it was a fine ould place, in the ould ancient times". In noticing the difference between the two round towers—for there are two very fine ones at Clonmacnoise, one on the top of the hill, and one close beside the plashy bank of the river—he accounted for the difference by a piece of legendary information with which he favoured me and which may, perhaps, prove of sufficient importance to interest the reader.

"You see, sir," said he, "the one down there beyant, at the river side, was built the first, and finished complate entirely, for the roof is an it, you see. But when that was built, the bishop thought that another id look very purty on the hill beyant, and so he bid the masons set to work, and build up another tower there.

"Well, away they went to work, as busy as nailers; troth it was jist like a bee-hive, every man with his hammer in his hand, and sure the tower was complated in due time.

"Well, when the last stone was laid on the roof, the bishop axes the masons how much he was to pay them, and they ups and towld him their price. But the bishop, they say, was a neygar [niggard]—God forgi' me for saying the word of so holy a man!— and he said they axed too much, and he wouldn't pay them. With that, my jew'l, the masons said they would take no less; and what would you think, but the bishop had the cunnin' to take away the ladthers that was reared up agin the tower.

" 'And now,' says he, 'my gay fellows,' says he, 'the divil a down out o' that you'll come antil you larn manners, and take what's offered to yees,' says he. 'And when yees come down in your price you may come down yourselves into the bargain.'

"Well, sure enough, he kep his word, and wouldn't let man nor mortyel go nigh them to help them. And faiks, the masons didn't like the notion of losing their honest airnins, and small blame to them. But sure they wor starvin' all the same and didn't know what in the wide world to do, when there was a fool chanced to pass by, and seen them.

" 'Musha! but you look well there,' says the innocent. 'An' how are you?' says he.

" 'Not much the betther av your axin,' says they.

" 'Maybe you're out there,' says he. So he questioned them, and they tould him how it was with them, and how the bishop tuk away the ladthers, and they couldn't come down.

" 'Tut, you fools,' says he. 'Sure isn't it asier to take down two stones nor to put up one?'

"Wasn't that mighty cute o' the fool, sir? And wid that, my dear sowl, no sooner said than done. Faiks, the masons began to pull down their work, and whin they went an for some time, the bishop bid them stop, and he'd let them down; but faiks, before he gev in to them they had taken the roof clane off; and that's the raison that one tower has a roof, sir, and the other has none."

But before I had seen Clonmacnoise and its towers, I was intimate with the most striking of its legends, by favour of the sinewy boatman who rowed me to it. We had not long left Shannonbridge when, doubling an angle of the shore and stretch-ing up a reach of the river where it widens, the principal round tower of Clonmacnoise became visible.

"What tower is that?" said I to my Charon.

"That's the big tower of Clonmacnoise, sir," he answered. "An', if your honour looks sharp a little to the right of it, lower down, you'll see the ruins of the ould palace."

On a somewhat closer inspection, I did perceive the remains he spoke of, dimly discernible in the distance; and it was not without his indication of their relative situation to the tower that I could have distinguished them from the sober grey of the horizon behind them, for the evening was closing fast, and we were moving eastward.

"Does your honour see it yit?" said my boatman.

"I do," said I.

"God spare you your eyesight," responded he, "for troth it's few gintleman could see the ould palace this far off, and the sun so low, barrin' they were used to spottin', and had a sharp eye for the birds over a bog, or the like o' that. Oh, then it's Clonmacnoise, your honour, that's the holy place," continued he. "Mighty holy in the ould ancient times, and mighty great too, wid the sivin churches, let alone the two towers, and the bishop, and plinty o' priests, and all to that."

"Two towers?" said I. "Then I suppose one has fallen?"

"Not at all, sir," said he, "but the other one that you can't see, is beyant in the hollow by the river side."

"And it was a great place, you say, in the ould ancient times?"

"Troth it was, sir, and is still, for to this day it bates the world in regard o' pilgrims."

"Pilgrims!" I ejaculated.

"Yes, sir," said the boatman, with his own quiet manner; although it was evident to a quick observer that my surprise at the mention of pilgrims had not escaped him.

I mused a moment. Pilgrims, thought I, in the British dominions, in the nineteenth century—strange enough!

"And so," continued I aloud, "you have pilgrims at Clonmacnoise?"

"Troth we have, your honour, from the top of the north and the farthest corner of Kerry. And may you see them any day in the week, let alone the pathern [patron] day, when all the world, you'd think, was there."

"And the palace," said I, "I suppose belonged to the bishop of Clonmacnoise?"

"Some says 'twas the bishop, your honour, and indeed it is them that has larnin' says so. But more says 'twas a King had it long ago, afore the churches was there at all, at all. And sure enough it looks far oulder nor the churches though them is ould enough in all conscience. All the knowledge people I ever heerd talk of it, says that. And now, sir," said he in an expostulatory tone, "wouldn't it be far more nath'ral that the bishop id live in the churches? And sure," continued he, evidently leaning to the popular belief, "it stands to raison that a King id live in a palace, and why shud it be called a palace if a King didn't live there?"

Satisfying himself with this most logical conclusion, he pulled his oar with evident self-complacency. As I have always found, I derived more legendary information by yielding somewhat to the narrator, and by abstaining from inflicting any wound on his pride by endeavouring to combat his credulity. I seemed to favour his conclusions, and admitted that a King must have been the former occupant of the palace.

So much being settled, he proceeded to tell me that "there was a mighty quare story" about the last King that ruled Clonmacnoise and, pulling his oar with an easier sweep lest he might disturb the quiet hearing of his legend, he prepared to tell his tale.

"Well, sir, they say there was a King wanst lived in the palace beyant and a sportin' fellow he was, and 'Cead mile failte' was the word in the palace; no one kem but was welkem, and I go bail the sorra one left it without the 'deoch an' doris'. Well, to be sure, the King av coorse had the best of eatin' and drinkin', and there was bed and boord for the stranger, let alone the welkim for the neighbour—and a good neighbour he was, by all accounts. Until, as bad luck would have it, a crass ould bishop (the saints forgi' me for saying the word) kem to rule over the churches. Now, you must know, the King was a likely man and, as I said already, he was a sportin' fellow, and by coorse a great favourite with the women; he had a smile and a wink for the crathers at every hand's turn, and the soft word, and the—the short and the long of it is, he was the divil among the girls.

"Well, sir, it was all mighty well, untell the ould bishop I mentioned arrived at the churches; but whin he kem, he tuck great scandal at the goings-an of the King, and he determined to cut him short in his coorses all at wanst. So with that whin the King wint to his duty, the bishop ups and he tells him that he must mend his manners, and all to that; and when the King said that the likes o' that was never tould him afore by the best priest o' them all, 'More shame for them that wor before me,' says the bishop.

"But to make a long story short, the King looked mighty black at the bishop, and the bishop looked twice blacker at him again, and so on, from bad to worse, till they parted the bittherest of inimies. And the King that was the best o' friends to the churches afore, swore be this and be that, he'd vex them for it, and that he'd be even with the bishop afore long.

"Now, sir, the bishop might jist as well have kept never minding the King's little kimneens with the girls, for the story goes that he had a little failin' of his own in regard of a dhrop, and that he knew the differ betune wine and wather, for, poor ignorant crathurs, it's little they knew about whiskey in them days.

"Well, the King used often to send lashins o' wine to the

churches, by the way, as he said, that they should have plinty of it for celebrating the Mass. He knew well that it was a little of it went far that-a-way, and that their Riverinces was fond of a hearty glass as well as himself. And why not, sir, if they'd let him alone?

" 'For,' says the King, as many a one said afore, and will again, 'I'll make a child's bargain with you,' says he. 'Do you let me alone, and I'll let you alone.' Manin' by that, sir, that if they'd say nothin' about the girls, he would give them plenty of wine.

"So it fell out a little before he had the scrimmage with the bishop, the King promised them a fine store of wine that was comin' up the Shannon in boats, sir. And big boats they wor, I'll go bail, not all as one as the little drolleen [wren] of a thing we're in now, but high-hand as big as a ship. And there was three of these fine boats full comin'—two for himself, and one for the churches.

"So says the King to himself, 'The divil receave the dhrop of that wine they shall get,' says he, 'the dirty beggarly neygars. Bad cess to the dhrop,' says he, 'my big-bellied bishop, to nourish your jolly red nose. I said I'd be even with you,' says he, 'and so I will. And if you spoil my divarshin, I'll spoil yours, and turn about is fair play, as the divil said to the smoke-jack.'

"With that, sir, the King goes and he gives ordhers to his sarvants how it wid be when the boats kem up the river with the wine—and more especial to one in partic'lar they called Corny, his own man, by raison he was mighty stout, and didn't love priest much more nor himself.

"Now Corny, sir, let alone bein' stout, was mighty dark, and if he wanst said the word, you might as well sthrive to move the rock of Dunamaise as Corny, though without a big word at all, at all, but as quite [quiet] as a child.

"Well, in good time, up kem the boats, and down runs the monks, all as one as a flock o' crows over a corn-field, to pick up whatever they could for themselves; but troth the King was afore them, for all his men was there with Corny at their head.

" 'Dominus vobiscum'—which manes, 'God save you,' sir— says one of the monks to Corny. 'We kem down to save you the throuble of unloadin' the wine, which the King, God bless him, gives to the church.'

" 'Oh, no trouble in life, plaze your Riverince,' says Corny, 'we'll unload it ourselves, your Riverince,' says he.

"With that they began unloadin', first one boat, and then another; but sure enough, every individual cashk of it went up to the palace, and not a one to the churches. So whin they seen the second boat a'most empty, quare thoughts began to come into their heads, for before this offer, the first boatload was always sent to the bishop, afore a dhrop was taken to the King, which, you know, was good manners, sir—and the king, by all accounts, was a gintleman, every inch of him.

"With that, says one of the monks: 'My blessin' an you, Corny, my son,' says he. 'Sure it's not forgettin' the bishop you'd be, nor the churches,' says he, 'that stands betune you and the Divil?'

"Well, sir, at the word Divil, 'twas as good as a play to see the look Corny gave out o' the corner of his eye at the monk.

" 'Forget yez?' says Corny. 'Troth it's long afore me or my masther,' says he—nodding his head a bit at the word—'will forget the bishop of Clonmacnoise. Go an with your work, boys,' says he to the men about him, and away they wint, and soon finished unloadin' the second boat. And with that they began at the third.

" 'God bless your work, boys,' says the bishop—for, sure enough, 'twas the bishop himself kem down to the river side, having got the hard word of what was goin' an. 'God bless your work,' says he, as they heaved the first barrel of wine out of the boat. 'Go, help them, my sons,' says he, turnin' round to half a dozen strappin' young priests as was standing by.

" 'No occasion in life, plaze your Riverince,' says Corny. 'I'm intirely obleeged to your lordship, but we're able for the work ourselves,' says he. And without sayin' another word, away went the barrel out of the boat, and up on their shoulders, or whatever way they wor takin' it, and up the hill to the palace.

" 'Hillo!' says the bishop. 'Where are yiz goin' with that wine?' says he.

" 'Where I tould them,' says Corny.

" 'Is it to the palace?' says his Riverince.

" 'Faith, you jist hit it,' says Corny.

" 'And what's that for?' says the bishop.

" 'For fun,' says Corny, no way frikened at all by the dark look the bishop gave him. And sure it's a wondher the fear of the Church didn't keep him in dread—but Corny was the divil intirely.

" 'Is that the answer you give your clergy, you reprobate?' says the bishop. 'I'll tell you what it is, Corny,' says he. 'As sure as you're standin' there I'll excommunicate you, my fine fellow, if you don't keep a civil tongue in your head.'

64

" 'Sure it wouldn't be worth your Riverince's while,' says Corny, 'to excommunicate the likes o' me,' says he, 'while there's the King my masther to the fore, for your Holiness to play bell, book, and candle-light with.'

" 'Do you mane to say, you scruff o' the earth,' says the bishop, 'that your masther, the King, put you up to what you're doing?'

" 'Divil a thing else I mane,' says Corny.

" 'You villain!' says the bishop. 'The King never did the like.'

" 'Yes, but I did though,' says the King, puttin' in his word fair and aisy, for he was lookin' out o' his dhrawin'-room windy, and had run down the hill to the river, when he seen the bishop goin', as he thought, to put his comether upon Corny.

" 'So,' says the bishop, turnin' round quite short to the King, 'so, my lord,' says he, 'am I to understand this villian has your commands for his purty behaviour?'

" 'He has my commands for what he has done,' says the King, quite stout. 'And more to be token, I'd have you to know he's no villain at all,' says he, 'but a thrusty sarvant, who does his masther's biddin'.'

" 'And don't you intind sendin' any of this wine over to my churches beyant?' says the bishop.

" 'Bad luck to the dhrop,' says the King.

" 'And what for?' says the bishop.

" 'Bekase I've changed my mind,' says the King.

" 'And won't you give the Church wine for the holy Mass?' says the bishop.

" 'The Mass!' says the King, eyein' him mighty sly.

" 'Yes, sir—the Mass,' says his Riverince, colouring up to the eyes, 'the Mass.'

" 'Oh, baithershin,' says the King.

" 'What do you mane?' says the bishop—and his nose got blue with rage.

" 'Oh, nothin',' says the King, with a toss of his head.

" 'Are you a gintleman?' says the bishop.

" 'Every inch o' me,' says the King.

" 'Then sure no gintleman goes back of his word,' says the other.

"I won't go back o' my word, either,' says the King. 'I promised to give wine for the Mass,' says he, 'and so I will. Send to my palace every Sunday mornin', and you shall have a bottle of wine, and that's plinty. For I'm thinkin',' says the King, 'that so much wine lyin' beyant there, is neither good for your bodies nor your sowls.'

" 'What do you mane?' says the bishop in a great passion, for all the world like a turkey-cock.

" 'I mane, that when your wine-cellar is so full,' says the King, 'it only brings the fairies about you, and makes away with the wine too fast,' says he laughin'. 'And for the fairies to be about the churches isn't good, your Riverince,' says the King. 'For I'm thinkin',' says he, 'that some of the spiteful little divils has given your Riverince a blast, and burnt the ind of your nose.'

"With that, my dear, you couldn't hould the bishop, with the rage he was in, and says he, 'You think to dhrink all that wine—but you're mistaken,' says he. 'Fill your cellars as much as you like,' says the bishop, 'but you'll die in drooth yit.'

"With that he went down on his knees and cursed the King—God betune us and harm!—and shakin' his fist at him, he gother [gathered] all his monks about him, and away they wint home to the churches.

"Well, sir, sure enough, the King fell sick of a sudden, and all the docthors in the country round was sent for, but they could do him no good at all, at all. Day by day he was wastin' and wastin', and pinin' and pinin', till the flesh was worn off his bones, and he was as bare and yellow as a kite's claw. Then, what would you think, but the drooth came an him sure enough, and he was callin' for dhrink every minit, till you'd think he'd dhrink the sae dhry.

"Well, when the clock struck twelve that night, the drooth was an him worse nor ever, though he dhrunk as much that day—ay, troth, as much as would turn a mill; and he called to his servants for a drink of grule [gruel].

" 'The grule's all out,' says they.

" 'Well, then give me some whay,' says he.

" 'There's none left, my lord,' says they.

" 'Then give me a dhrink of wine,' says he.

" 'There's none in the room, dear,' says the nurse-tindher.

" 'Then go down to the wine-cellar,' says he, 'and get some.'

"With that, they wint to the wine-cellar—but, jew'l machree, they soon run back into his room, with their faces as white as a sheet, and told him there was not one dhrop of wine in all the cashks in the cellar.

" 'Oh murther! murther!' says the King, 'I'm dyin' of drooth,' say he.

"And then—God help iz!—they bethought themselves of what the bishop said, and the curse he laid an the King.

67

" 'You've no grule?' says the King.

" 'No,' says they.

" 'Nor whay?'

" 'No,' says the sarvants.

" 'Nor wine?' says the King.

" 'Nor wine either, my Lord,' says they.

" 'Have you no tay?' says he.

" 'Not a dhrop,' says the nurse-tindher.

" 'Then,' says the King, 'for the tindher marcy of heaven, gi' me a dhrink of wather.'

"And what would you think, sir, but there wasn't a dhrop of wather in the palace.

" 'Oh, murther, murther!' says the King. 'Isn't it a poor case, that a King can't get a dhrink of wather in his own house? Go then,' says he, 'and get me a jug of wather out of the ditch.'

"For there was a big ditch, sir, round the palace. And away they run for wather out of the ditch, while the King was roarin' like mad for the drooth, and his mouth like a coal of fire. And sure, sir, as the story goes, they coundn't find any wather in the ditch!

" 'Millia murther! Millia murther!' cries the King. 'Will no one take pity an a King that's dyin' for the bare drooth?'

"And they thrimbled again, with the fair fright, when they heerd this, and thought of the ould bishop's prophecy.

" 'Well,' says the poor King, 'run down to the Shannon,' says he, 'and sure, at all events, you'll get wather there,' says he.

"Well, sir, away they run with pails and noggins down to the Shannon, and—God betune us and harm!—what do you think, sir, but the river Shannon was dhry! So, av coors, when the King heerd the Shannon was gone dhry, it wint to his heart; and he thought o' the bishop's curse an him—and, givin' one mutherin' big screech, that split the walls of the palace, as may be seen to this day, he died, sir—makin' the bishop's words good, that 'he would die of drooth yet'.

"And now, sir," says my historian, with a look of lurking humour in his dark grey eye, "isn't that mighty wondherful? In it's thrue."

Fin MacCumhail and the Son of the King of Alba

BY JEREMIAH CURTIN

n a day Fin went out hunting with his dog Bran, on Knock an Ar, and he killed so much game that he didn't know what to do with it or how to bring it home. As he stood looking and thinking, all at once he saw a man running towards him, with a rope around his waist so long that half his body was covered with it; and the man was of such size that, as he ran, Fin could see the whole world between his legs and nothing between his head and the sky. When he came up, the man saluted Fin, who answered him most kindly. "Where are you going?" asked Fin.

"I am out looking for a master."

"Well," said Fin, "I am in sore need of a man. What can you do?"

"Do you see this rope on my body? Whatever this rope will bind, I can carry."

"If that is true," said Fin, "you are the man I want. Do you see the game on this hillside?"

"I do," said the man.

"Well, put that into the rope and carry it to my castle."

The man put all the game into the rope, made a great bundle, and threw it on his back.

"Show me the way to the castle now," said he.

Fin started on ahead, and though he ran with all his might, he could not gain one step on the man who followed with the game. The sentry on guard at the castle saw the man running while yet far off. He stepped inside the gate and said: "There is a man coming with a load on his back as big as a mountain." Before he could come out again to his place the man was there and the load

69

off his back. When the game came to the ground, it shook the castle to its foundations.

Next day the man was sent to herd cows for a time, and while he was gone, Conan Maol said to Fin: "If you don't put this cow-herd to death, he will destroy all the Fenians of Erin."

"How could I put such a good man to death?" asked Fin.

"Send him," said Conan, "to sow corn on the brink of a lake in the north of Erin. Now, in that lake lives a serpent that never lets a person pass, but swallows every man that goes that way."

Fin agreed to this, and the next morning after breakfast he called the man, gave him seven bullocks, a plough, and a sack of grain, and sent him to the lake in the north of Erin to sow corn.

When the man came to the lake, he started to plough, drew one furrow. The lake began to boil up, and as he was coming back, making the second furrow, the serpent was on the field before him and swallowed the seven bullocks and the plough up to the handles. But the man held fast to what he had in his two hands, gave a pull, and dragged the plough and six of the bullocks out of the belly of the serpent. The seventh one remained inside. The serpent went at him and they fought for seven days and nights. At the end of that time the serpent was as tame as a cat, and the man drove him and the six bullocks home before him.

When he was in sight of Fin's castle, the sentry at the gate ran in and cried: "That cowherd is coming with the size of a mountain before him!"

"Run out," said Conan Maol, "and tell him to tie the serpent to that oak out there."

They ran out, and the man tied the serpent to the oak tree, then came in and had a good supper.

Next morning the man went out to herd cows as before. "Well," said Conan Maol to Fin, "if you don't put this man to death, he'll destroy you and me and all the Fenians of Erin."

"How could I put such a man to death?"

"There is," said Conan, "a bullock in the north of Erin, and he drives fog out of himself for seven days and then he draws it in for seven other days. Tomorrow is the last day for drawing it in. If any one man comes near, he'll swallow him alive."

When the cowherd came to supper in the evening, Fin said to him: "I am going to have a feast and need fresh beef. Now there is a bullock in that same valley by the lake in the north of Erin where you punished the serpent and if you go there and bring the bullock to me, you'll have my thanks."

"I'll go," said the man, "the first thing after breakfast in the morning."

So off he went next morning, and when he came near the valley, he found the bullock asleep and drawing in the last of the fog. Soon he found himself going in with it. So he caught hold of a great oak-tree for safety. The bullock woke up then and saw him, and letting a roar out of himself, faced him, and gave him a pitch with his horn which sent him seven miles over the top of a wood. And when he fell to the ground, the bullock was on him again before he had time to rise, and gave him another pitch which sent him back and broke three ribs in his body.

"This will never do," said the man, as he rose and, pulling up an oak tree by the roots for a club, he faced the bullock. And there they were at one another for five days and nights, till the bullock was as tame as a cat and the man drove him home to Fin's castle.

The sentry saw them coming and ran inside the gate with word.

"Tell the man to tie the bullock to that oak tree beyond," said Conan. "We don't want him near this place."

The cowherd tied the bullock, and told Fin to send four of the best butchers in Erin to kill him with an axe; and the four of them struck him one after another and any of them couldn't knock him.

"Give me an axe," said the man to the butchers. They gave him the axe, and the first stroke he gave, he knocked the bullock. Then they began to skin him, but the man didn't like the way they were doing the work, so he took his sword and had three quarters of the bullock skinned before they could skin one.

Next morning the cowherd went out with the cows, but he wasn't long gone when Conan Maol came to Fin and said: "If you don't put an end to that man, he'll soon put an end to you and to me and to all of us, so there won't be a man of the Fenians of Erin left alive."

"How could I put an end to a man like him?" asked Fin.

"There is in the north of Erin," said Conan, "a wild sow who has two great pigs of her own. She and her two pigs have bags of poison in their tails, and when they see any man, they run at him and shake their poison bags; and if the smallest drop of the poison touches him, it is death to him that minute. If by any chance he should escape the wild sow and the pigs, there is a fox-man called the Gruagach, who has but one eye and that in the middle of his forehead. The Gruagach carries a club of a ton weight, and if the cowherd gets one welt of that club, he'll never trouble the Fenians of Erin again."

Next morning Fin called up the cowherd and said: "I am going to have a feast in this castle, and I would like to have some fresh pork. There is a wild sow in the north of Erin with two pigs, and if you bring her to me before the feast, you'll have my thanks."

"I'll go and bring her to you," said the cowherd.

So after breakfast he took his sword, went to the north of Erin, and stole up to the sow and two pigs, and whipped the tails off the three of them, before they knew he was in it. Then he faced the wild sow and fought with her for four days and five nights, and on the morning of the fifth day he knocked her dead. At the last blow, his sword stuck in her backbone and he couldn't draw it out. But with one pull he broke the blade, and stood there over her with only the hilt in his hand. Then he put his foot on one of her jaws, took the other in his hands and, splitting her evenly from the nose to the tail, made two halves of her.

He threw one half on his shoulder; and that minute the big Gruagach with one eye in his head came along and made an offer of his club at him to kill him. But the cowherd jumped aside, and catching the Gruagach by one of his legs, threw him up on to the half of the wild sow on his shoulder, and taking the other half of her from the ground, clapped that on the top of the Gruagach, and ran away to Fin's castle as fast as his legs could carry him.

The sentry at the castle gate ran in and said: "The cowherd is running to the castle, and the size of a mountain on his back."

"Go out now," said Conan Maol, "and stop him where he is, or he'll throw down the castle if he comes here with the load that's on him."

But before the sentry was back at his place, the cowherd was at the gate shaking the load off his back and the castle to its foundations, so that every dish and vessel in it was broken to bits.

The Gruagach jumped from the ground, rubbed his legs and every part of him that was sore from the treatment he got. He was so much in dread of the cowherd that he ran with all the strength that was in him, and never stopped to look back till he was in the north of Erin.

Next morning the cowherd went out with the cows, drove them back in the evening; and while picking the thigh-bone of a bullock for his supper, Oscar, son of Oisin, the strongest man of the Fenians of Erin, came up to him and took hold of the bone to pull it from his hand. The cowherd held one end and Oscar the other, and pulled till they made two halves of the bone.

"What did you carry away?" asked the cowherd.

"What I have in my hand," said Oscar.

"And I kept what I held in my fist," said the cowherd.

"There is that for you now," said Oscar, and he hit him a slap.

The cowherd said no word in answer, but next morning he asked his wages of Fin.

"Oh, then," said Fin, "I'll pay you and welcome, for you are the best man I have ever had or met with."

Then the cowherd went away to Cahirciveen in Kerry where he had an enchanted castle. But before he went he invited Fin MacCumhail and the Fenians of Erin to have a great feast with him. "For," said he to Fin, "I'm not a cowherd at all, but the son of the King of Alba, and I'll give you good cheer."

When the Fenians came to the place, they found the finest castle that could be seen. There were three fires in each room and seven spits at every fire. When they had gone and sat down in their places, there was but one fire in each room.

"Rise up, every man of you," said Fin, "or we are lost; for this is an enchanted place."

They tried to rise, but each man was fastened to his seat, and the seat to the floor; and not one of them could stir. Then the last fire went out and they were in darkness.

"Chew your thumb," said Conan to Fin, "and try is there any way out of here."

Fin chewed his thumb and knew what trouble they were in. Then he put his two hands into his mouth and blew the old-time whistle. And this whistle was heard by Pogan and Ceolan, two sons of Fin who were in the North at that time, one fishing and the other hurling.

When they heard the whistle, they said: "Our father and the Fenians of Erin are in trouble." And they faced towards the sound and never stopped till they knocked at the door of the enchanted castle of the son of Alba at Cahirciveen.

"Who is there?" asked Fin.

"Your two sons," said one of them.

"Well," said Fin, "we are in danger of death tonight. That cowherd I had in my service was no cowherd at all, but the son of the King of Alba, and his father has said that he will not eat three meals off one table without having my head. There is an army now on the road to kill us tonight. There is no way in or out of this castle but by one ford, and to that ford the army of the King of Alba is coming."

The two sons of Fin went out at nightfall and stood in the ford before the army. The son of the King of Alba knew them well, and calling each by name, said: "Won't you let us pass?"

"We will not," said they; and then the fight began. The two sons of Fin MacCumhail, Pogan and Ceolan, destroyed the whole army and killed every man except the son of the King of Alba.

After the battle the two went back to their father. "We have destroyed the whole army at the ford," said they.

"There is a greater danger ahead," said Fin. "There is an old hag coming with a little pot. She will dip her finger in the pot, touch the lips of the dead men, and bring the whole army to life. But first of all there will be music at the ford, and if you hear the music, you'll fall asleep. Now go, but if you do not overpower the old hag, we are lost."

"We'll do the best we can," said the two sons of Fin.

They were not long at the ford when one said: "I am falling asleep from that music."

"So am I," said the other.

"Knock your foot down on mine," said the first.

The other kicked his foot and struck him, but no use. Then each took his spear and drove it through the foot of the other, but both fell asleep in spite of the spears.

The old hag went on touching the lips of the dead men, who stood up alive, and she was crossing the ford at the head of the army when she stumbled over the two sleeping brothers and spilt what was in the pot over their bodies.

They sprang up fresh and well, and picking up two stones of a ton weight each that were there in the ford, they made for the champions of Alba and never stopped till they killed the last man of them. Then they killed the old hag herself.

Pogan and Ceolan then knocked at the door of the castle.

"Who's there?" asked Fin.

"Your two sons," said they. "And we have killed all the champions of Alba and the old hag as well."

"You have more to do yet," said Fin. "There are three kings in the north of Erin who have three silver goblets. These kings are holding a feast in a fort today. You must go and cut the heads off the three, put their blood in the goblets and bring them here. When you come, rub the blood on the keyhole of the door and it will open before you. When you come in, rub the seats and we shall all be free."

The three goblets of blood were brought to Cahirciveen, the door of the castle flew open, and light came into every room. The

75

brothers rubbed blood on the chairs of all the Fenians of Erin and freed them all, except Conan Maol, who had no chair, but sat on the floor with his back to the wall. When they came to him the last drop of blood was gone.

All the Fenians of Erin were hurrying past, anxious to escape, and paid no heed to Conan, who had never a good word in his mouth for any man. Then Conan turned to Diarmuid, and said: "If a woman were here in place of me, you wouldn't leave her to die this way."

Then Diarmuid turned, took him by one hand, and Goll MacMorna by the other and, pulling with all their might, tore him from the wall and the floor. But as they did, he left all the skin of his back from his head to his heels on the floor and the wall behind him. But when they were going home through the hills of Tralee, they found a sheep on the way, killed it, and clapped the skin on Conan. The sheepskin grew to his body and he was so well and strong that they sheared him every year, and got wool enough from his back to make flannel and frieze for the Fenians of Erin ever after.

The Fianna

TRANSLATED BY
STANDISH HAYES O'GRADY

*t*his is the enumeration of Finn's people. Their strength was seven-score-and-ten officers, each man of these having thrice nine warriors, every one bound (as was the way with Cuchulainn in the time when he was there) to certain conditions of service. Namely that in satisfaction of a guarantee violated they must not accept material compensation in the matter of valuables or of meat; must not deny any guarantee; nor any single individual of them fly before warriors.

Not a man was taken into the Fianna nor admitted whether to the great Gathering of Usnach, to the Convention of Taillte, or to Tara's Feast, until both his paternal and his maternal co-relatives, his tuatha and kindreds, had given securities for him to the effect that though at the present instant he were slain, yet should not claim be urged in lieu of him. This in order that to none other but to themselves alone should the Fianna look to avenge themselves. On the other hand, in the case it were they inflicted great mischiefs upon others, reprisals were not to be made upon their relatives.

Again not a man was taken until he was a prime poet versed in the twelve books of poetic composition. No man was taken till in the ground a large hole had been made (such as to reach the fold of his belt) and he put into it with his shield and a forearm's length of a hazel stick. Then must nine warriors, having nine spears, with a ten furrows' width betwixt them and him, assail him and in concert let fly at him. If past that guard of his he were hurt then, he was not received into Fianship.

Not a man of them was taken till his hair had been interwoven into braids on him and he started at a run through Ireland's woods; while they, seeking to wound him, followed in his wake, there having been between him and them but one forest bough

77

by way of interval at first. Should he be overtaken, he was wounded and not received into the Fianna after. If his weapons had quivered in his hand, he was not taken. Should a branch in the wood have disturbed anything of his hair out of its braiding, neither was he taken. If he had cracked a dry stick under his foot as he ran, he was not accepted. Unless that at full speed he had both jumped a stick level with his brow and stooped to pass under one even with his knee, he was not taken. Also, unless without slackening his pace he could with his nail extract a thorn from his foot, he was not taken into Fianship. But if he performed all this he was of Finn's people.

15th or 16th CENTURY

Diarmuid and Grainne

ADAPTED BY MARY McGARRY

On the death of his wife, Manissa, the daughter of Garad of the Black Knee, Finn MacCumhail sought the hand of the young and beautiful daughter of King Cormac MacArt called Grainne. The King approved of the match and feasted Finn and his Fianna men at Tara. However, during the celebrations it chanced that Grainne sat next to Diarmuid, one of Finn's bravest warriors, renowned for his courage and high-mindedness.

Now, since the fair Grainne felt nothing for Finn, who was indeed even older than her own father, she appealed to Diarmuid to save her from a hateful marriage, having at first sight fallen deeply in love with the young hero.

Diarmuid was greatly disturbed for he could not help loving the princess with all his heart, but he wished to hide this as he put his duty to his chief above all else. However, seeing this, Grainne placed Diarmuid under a "geasa" and under bonds of heavy druidical spells—bonds that true heroes never break through—to take her away before Finn and the rest awoke for the wedding.

Diarmuid sought advice from his friends; of these even Oisin, the son of Finn, said that under such a bond he should leave Tara with the princess, but forever beware of the wrath of Finn.

So Diarmuid and Grainne plighted their faith and vowed solemnly to be true to each other as man and wife for ever.

The couple fled from Tara, first by chariot as far as the ford of Athlone, where Diarmuid carried Grainne across the water and they continued on foot. When they reached the Wood of the Two Tents, Diarmuid built a hut of branches where the couple rested.

Meanwhile Finn, burning with jealousy and rage, ordered the

F

tracking-men, the Clann Navin, to pursue them. When all tracks disappeared at Athlone, Finn in a fit of anger told the trackers that unless they took up the track again speedily, he would hang every man of the Clann Navin on the edge of the ford.

When the pursuers came to the Wood of the Two Tents, it seemed certain that Diarmuid and his love would be discovered. But Oisin and others who cared for Diarmuid sent Finn's hound, Bran, to warn him of the approach of the Fianna.

However, despite Grainne's fears, Diarmuid refused to flee till Finn had overtaken them. For the hero had cleared a space round the hut and surrounded it with a fence that no man could pierce, with seven narrow doors of strong poles woven with saplings, to face seven different parts of the wood. Finn stationed his men around the fence to wait for the couple to attempt to escape.

Now Angus of Brugh, the wisest and the most skilled in magic arts of all the Dedannan race, was Diarmuid's foster-father. He had taught him all the arts and accomplishments of a champion and loved him as a father does his only son. It was revealed to Angus that Diarmuid was in great danger, so he arose and travelled on the wings of the east wind to the Wood of the Two Tents, and entered the hut without being perceived by Finn and his men. Diarmuid warmly greeted the old man, and on hearing their story Angus summoned the pair to escape under his mantle, without Finn's knowledge. But Diarmuid was determined to stay and face Finn. If he should be slain he asked that Grainne be restored to her father. Angus then took Grainne safely away as far as the Wood of the Two Sallows, now called Limerick.

Diarmuid girded on his armour, and marched, weapon in hand, to one of the seven narrow doors and asked who was outside. Oisin and Oscar replied that it was they who guarded this door and that he had nothing to fear from them. But Diarmuid wished to find the door which Finn himself guarded. At the second and third doors more friends promised to help him, but Diarmuid repeated that he would not go out as it would only bring Finn's displeasure on those that acted kindly to him. At one door the Clann Navin threatened him with their spears, but he went on until he reached the door behind which Finn himself stood. At that door, Diarmuid found an unguarded place, rose by means of his two spears with a light, airy bound over the fence and landed on the clear space outside. Running swiftly, he was soon out of reach of sword and spear. Happily he sped towards the Wood of the Two Sallows and rejoined his princess.

However Angus realised that Finn would still seek the couple and counselled them well as to what they should do before he left them. Indeed Diarmuid and Grainne had many more adventures and perils to face in their flight from the revenge of Finn; local people still point out their resting places of refuge, called the "Beds of Diarmuid and Grainne".

Finally Angus went to Finn and asked him to make peace with Diarmuid. Finn, seeing he could not overcome the hero, told Angus he was weary of the quarrel and ready to agree to peace on whatever terms Diarmuid chose. King Cormac was also ready to forgive his son-in-law and give his other daughter to Finn as a wife.

Diarmuid and Grainne settled far away from both Finn and Cormac on land granted to them, and their family grew in number and prosperity as the years went by. But one day Grainne, sad to be so far removed from the world, asked Diarmuid that her father and Finn might visit their house. Unluckily Diarmuid consented and a great feast was held for the guests.

One night, Diarmuid heard the call of a hound and wished to investigate the sound that thus disturbed the night. Grainne in fear cautioned him, but the next day Diarmuid would be held back no longer, regardless of any danger that Grainne's heart foretold. Diarmuid set out and came to the summit of Ben-Gulben, where he found Finn. The Fianna were chasing the wild boar of Ben-Gulben which, having already slain many of his pursuers, was heading towards the very hillock where the two men stood.

Diarmuid was not likely to flee before a mere boar, but Finn told Diarmuid that, although he did not know it, he was under a "geasa" never to hunt a boar. The old warrior explained that a youth slain several years before by Donn, Diarmuid's father, was changed at the moment of his death into a druidic boar, and appointed to slay the son of his murderer. Angus had known this and commanded that the child should never hunt a wild boar.

Having said this, Finn parted from Diarmuid, who attacked the boar with his usual courage. But neither spear nor arm could harm the boar, and as he finally stood defenceless the animal gashed the warrior's side with his tusk, making a deep wound. Diarmuid prevented another attack by flinging his sword through the skull of the boar, who fell dead.

Finn and the Fianna arrived to find the hero bleeding to death. Diarmuid appealed to Finn to use his gift of healing to save him, by giving him a drink of water from the closed palms of his two

hands. Finn hesitated and Diarmuid recalled the times when he had helped his leader, but Finn could not forget Grainne and Diarmuid's betrayal at Tara.

Yet when all around him were moved to pity for the dying man, Finn at last went to a nearby well in search of water. But after he had walked a short way he let it spill through his fingers. Again he went to the well, but at the thought of Grainne the water spilt out yet once more. Finn was hastening forward for a third time when Diarmuid's head dropped back as he left this life.

Grainne and the Fianna wept for the man they loved so much, and Angus in deep grief that he had not been there to prevent the doom of his favourite son, carried the body of the dead hero to its last resting place near him at Brugh.

Oisin in Tir Na nOg
or The Last of the Fena

BY P. W. JOYCE

According to an ancient legend, Finn's son, Oisin, the hero-poet, survived to the time of St. Patrick, two hundred years (the legend makes it three hundred) after the other Fena. On a certain occasion, when the saint asked him how he had lived to such a great age, the old hero related the following story.

 short time after the fatal battle of Gavra, where so many of our heroes fell, we were hunting on a dewy morning near the brink of Loch Lein, where the trees and hedges around us were all fragrant with blossoms, and the little birds sang melodious music on the branches. We soon roused the deer from the thickets, and as they bounded over the plain, our hounds in full cry followed after them.

We were not long so engaged, when we saw a rider coming swiftly towards us from the west; and we soon perceived that it was a maiden on a white steed. We all ceased from the chase on seeing the lady, who reined in as she approached. And Finn and the Fena were greatly surprised, for they had never before seen so lovely a maiden. A slender golden diadem encircled her head. She wore a brown robe of silk, spangled with stars of red gold, which was fastened in front by a golden brooch, and fell from her shoulders till it swept the ground. Her yellow hair flowed far down over her robe in bright, golden ringlets. Her blue eyes were as clear as the drops of dew on the grass and while her small, white hand held the bridle and curbed her steed with a golden bit, she sat more gracefully than a swan on Loch Lein.

The white steed was covered with a smooth, flowing mantle. He was shod with four shoes of pure yellow gold, and in all Erin a better or more beautiful steed could not be found.

As she came slowly to the presence of Finn, he addressed her courteously: "Who art thou, O lovely youthful princess? Tell us thy name and the name of thy country, and relate to us the cause of thy coming."

She answered in a sweet and gentle voice: "Noble King of the Fena, I have had a long journey this day, for my country lies far off in the Western Sea. I am the daughter of the King of Tir na nOg, and my name is Niamh of the Golden Hair."

"And what is it that has caused thee to come so far across the sea? Has thy husband forsaken thee? Or what other evil has befallen thee?"

"My husband has not forsaken me, for I have never been married or betrothed to any man. But I love thy noble son, Oisin, and this is what has brought me to Erin. It is not without reason that I have given him my love, and that I have undertaken this long journey. For I have often heard of his bravery, his gentleness, and the nobleness of his person. Many princes and high chiefs have sought me in marriage, but I was quite indifferent to all men and never consented to wed, till my heart was moved with love for thy gentle son, Oisin."

When I heard these words, and when I looked on the lovely maiden with her glossy, golden hair, I was all over in love with her. I came near, and, taking her small hand in mine, I told her she was a mild star of brightness and beauty, and that I preferred her to all the princesses in the world for my wife.

"Then," said she, "I place you under 'geasa', which true heroes never break through, to come with me on my white steed to Tir na nOg, the land of never-ending youth. It is the most delightful and the most renowned country under the sun. There is abundance of gold and silver and jewels, of honey and wine; and the trees bear fruit and blossoms and green leaves together all the year round.

"You will get a hundred swords and a hundred robes of silk and satin, a hundred swift steeds, and a hundred slender, keen-scenting hounds. You will get herds of cows without number, flocks of sheep with fleeces of gold, a coat of mail that cannot be pierced, and a sword that never missed a stroke and from which no one ever escaped alive.

"There are feasting and harmless pastimes each day. A hundred warriors fully armed shall always await you at call, and harpers shall delight you with their sweet music. You will wear the diadem of the King of Tir na nOg, which he never yet gave to anyone under the sun, and which will guard you day and night, in tumult and battle and danger of every kind.

"Lapse of time shall bring neither decay nor death, and you shall be for ever young, and gifted with unfading beauty and strength. All these delights you shall enjoy, and many others that I do not mention; and I myself will be your wife if you come with me to Tir na nOg."

I replied that she was my choice above all the maidens in the world, and that I would willingly go with her to the Land of Youth.

When my father, Finn, and the Fena heard me say this, and knew that I was going from them, they raised three shouts of grief and lamentation. And Finn came up to me and took my hand in his, saying sadly: "Woe is me, my son, that you are going away from me, for I do not expect that you will ever return to me."

The manly beauty of his countenance became quite dimmed with sorrow, and though I promised to return after a little time, and fully believed that I should see him again, I could not check my tears as I gently kissed my father's cheek.

I then bade farewell to my dear companions, and mounted the white steed, while the lady kept her seat before me. She gave the signal, and the steed galloped swiftly and smoothly towards the west, till he reached the strand; and when his gold-shod hooves touched the waves, he shook himself and neighed three times. He made no delay, but plunged forward at once, moving over the face of the sea with the speed of a cloud-shadow on a March day. The wind overtook the waves and we overtook the wind, so that we straightway lost sight of land; and we saw nothing but billows tumbling before us and billows tumbling behind us.

Other shores came into view, and we saw many wonderful things on our journey—islands and cities, lime-white mansions, bright grianáns [summer houses] and lofty palaces. A hornless fawn once crossed our course, bounding nimbly along from the crest of one wave to the crest of another; and close after in full chase, a white hound with red ears. We saw also a lovely young maiden on a brown steed, with a golden apple in her hand; and as she passed swiftly by, a young warrior on a white steed plunged after her, wearing a long, flowing mantle of yellow silk, and holding a gold-hilted sword in his hand.

I knew naught of these things, and, marvelling much, I asked the princess what they meant.

"Heed not what you see here, Oisin," she said, "for all these wonders are as nothing compared with what you shall see in Tir na nOg."

At last we saw at a great distance, rising over the waves on the very verge of the sea, a palace more splendid than all the others; and, as we drew near, its front glittered like the morning sun. I asked the lady what royal house this was, and who was the prince that ruled over it.

"This country is the Land of Virtues," she replied. "Its King is the giant, Fomor of the Blows, and its Queen the daughter of the King of the Land of Life. This Fomor brought the lady away by force from her own country, and keeps her in his palace. But she has put him under 'geasa' that he cannot break through, never to ask her to marry him till she can find a champion to fight him in single combat. Yet she still remains in bondage, for no hero has yet come hither who has the courage to meet the giant."

"A blessing on you, golden-haired Niamh," I replied. "I have never heard music sweeter than your voice and although I feel pity for this princess, yet your story is pleasant to hear. Of a certainty I will go to the palace, and try whether I cannot kill this Fomor, and free the lady."

So we came to land, and as we drew nigh to the palace the lovely princess met us and bade us welcome. She led us in and placed us on chairs of gold. After which choice food was placed before us, and drinking-horns filled with mead, and golden goblets of sweet wine.

When we had eaten and drunk, the mild young princess told us her story, while tears streamed from her soft blue eyes. She ended by saying: "I shall never return to my own country and to my father's house, so long as this great and cruel giant is live."

When I heard her sad voice, and saw her tears falling, I was moved with pity. Telling her to cease from her grief, I gave her my hand as a pledge that I would meet the giant, and either slay him or fall myself in her defence.

While we were yet speaking, we saw the giant coming towards the palace, large of body and ugly and hateful in appearance, carrying a load of deerskins on his back and holding a great iron club in his hand. He threw down his load when he saw us, turned a surly look on the princess, and, without greeting us, or showing the least mark of courtesy, he forthwith challenged me to battle in a loud, rough voice.

It was not my wont to be dismayed by a call to battle, or to be terrified at the sight of an enemy, and I went forth at once without the least fear in my heart. But though I had fought many battles in Erin against wild boars and enchanters and foreign invaders, never before did I find it so hard to preserve my life. We fought for three days and three nights without food or drink or sleep, for the giant did not give me a moment for rest and neither did I give him. At length, when I looked at the two princesses weeping in great fear, and when I called to mind my father's deeds in battle, the fury of my valour arose. With a sudden onset I felled the giant to the earth and instantly, before he could recover himself, I cut off his head.

When the maidens saw the monster lying on the ground dead, they uttered three cries of joy and they came to me, and led me into the palace. For I was indeed bruised all over, and covered with gory wounds, and a sudden dizziness of brain and feebleness of body seized me. But the daughter of the King of the Land of Life applied precious balsam and healing herbs to my wounds and in a short time I was healed, and my cheerfulness of mind returned.

Then I buried the giant in a deep and wide grave and I raised a great carn over him, and placed on it a stone with his name graved in Ogham.

We rested that night, and at the dawn of next morning Niamh said to me that it was time for us to resume our journey to Tir na nOg. So we took leave of the daughter of the King of the Land of Life; and though her heart was joyful after her release, she wept at our departure, and we were not less sorry at parting from her. When we had mounted the white steed, he galloped towards the strand. As soon as his hooves touched the wave, he shook himself and neighed three times. We plunged forward over the clear, green sea with the speed of a March wind on a hillside. Soon we saw nothing but billows tumbling before us and billows tumbling behind us. We saw again the fawn chased by the white hound with red ears, and the maiden with the golden apple passed swiftly by, followed by the young warrior in yellow silk on his white steed. And again we passed many strange islands and cities and white palaces.

The sky now darkened, so that the sun was hidden from our view. A storm arose, and the sea was lighted up with constant flashes. But though the wind blew from every point of the heavens, and the waves rose up and roared around us, the white steed kept his course straight on, moving as calmly and swiftly as before, through the foam and blinding spray, without being delayed or disturbed in the least, and without turning either to the right or to the left.

At length the storm abated, and after a time the sun again shone brightly. When I looked up, I saw a country near at hand, all green and full of flowers, with beautiful smooth plains, blue hills, and bright lakes and waterfalls. Not far from the shore stood a palace of surpassing beauty and splendour. It was covered all over with gold and with gems of every colour—blue, green, crimson, and yellow. On each side were grianáns shining with precious stones, built by artists the most skilful that could be found.

I asked Niamh the name of that delightful country, and she replied: "This is my native country, Tir na nOg. And there is nothing I have promised you that you will not find in it."

As soon as we reached the shore, we dismounted; and now we saw advancing from the palace a troop of noble-looking warriors, all clad in bright garments, who came forward to meet and welcome us. Following these we saw a stately glittering host, with the King at their head wearing a robe of bright yellow satin covered with gems, and a crown that sparkled with gold and diamonds. The Queen came after, attended by a hundred lovely young maidens; and as they advanced towards us, it seemed to me that this King and Queen exceeded all the kings and queens of the world in beauty and gracefulness and majesty.

After they had kissed their daughter, the King took my hand, and said aloud in the hearing of the host: "This is Oisin, the son of Finn, for whom my daughter, Niamh, travelled over the sea to Erin. This is Oisin, who is to be the husband of Niamh of the Golden Hair. We give you a hundred thousand welcomes, brave Oisin. You will be forever young in this land. All kinds of delights and innocent pleasures are awaiting you, and my daughter, the gentle, golden-haired Niamh, shall be your wife, for I am King of Tir na nOg."

I gave thanks to the King, and I bowed low to the Queen; after which we went into the palace, where we found a banquet prepared. The feasting and rejoicing lasted for ten days, and on the last day I was wedded to the gentle Niamh of the Golden Hair.

I lived in the Land of Youth more than three hundred years, but it appeared to me that only three years had passed since the day I parted from my friends. At the end of that time, I began to have a longing desire to see my father, Finn, and all my old friends, and I asked leave of Niamh and of the King to visit Erin.

The King gave permission, and Niamh said: "I will give consent, though I feel sorrow in my heart, for I fear much you will never return to me."

I replied that I would surely return, and that she need not feel any doubt or dread, for that the white steed knew the way and would bring me back in safety. Then she addressed me in these words, which seemed very strange to me.

"I will not refuse this request, though your journey afflicts me with great grief and fear. Erin is not now as it was when you left it. The great King Finn and his Fena are all gone. You will find, instead of them, a holy father and hosts of priests and saints. Now, think well on what I say to you, and keep my words in your mind. If once you alight from the white steed, you will never come back to me. Again I warn you, if you place your feet on the green sod in Erin, you will never return to this lovely land. A third time, O Oisin, my beloved husband, a third time I say to you, if you alight from the white steed, you will never see me again."

I promised that I would faithfully attend to her words, and that I would not alight from the white steed. Then, as I looked into her gentle face and marked her grief, my heart was weighed down with sadness, and my tears flowed plentifully. But even so, my mind was bent on coming back to Erin.

When I had mounted the white steed, he galloped straight towards the shore. We moved as swiftly as before over the clear sea. The wind overtook the waves and we overtook the wind, so that we straightway left the Land of Youth behind. We passed by many islands and cities, till at length we landed on the green shores of Erin.

As I travelled on through the country, I looked closely around me, but I scarcely knew the old places, for everything seemed strangely altered. I saw no sign of Finn, and his host, and I began to dread that Niamh's saying was coming true. At length, I espied at a distance a company of little men and woman, all mounted on horses as small as themselves; and when I came near, they greeted me kindly and courteously. They looked at me with wonder and curiosity, and they marvelled much at my great size, and at the beauty and majesty of my person.

I asked them about Finn and the Fena—whether they were still living, or if any sudden disaster had swept them away. And one replied: "We have heard of the hero Finn, who ruled the Fena of Erin in times of old, and who never had an equal for bravery and wisdom. The poets of Gael have written many books concerning his deeds and the deeds of the Fena, which we cannot now relate, but they are gone long since, for they lived many ages ago. We have heard also, and we have seen it written in very old books, that Finn had a son named Oisin. Now this Oisin went with a young fairy maiden to Tir na nOg, and his father and his friends sorrowed greatly after him, and sought him long; but he was never seen again."

When I heard all this, I was filled with amazement, and my heart grew heavy with sorrow. I silently turned my steed from the wondering people, and set forward straightway for Allen of the mighty deeds, on the broad, green plains of Leinster. It was a miserable journey to me; and though my mind, being full of sadness at all I saw and heard, forecasted further sorrows, I was grieved more than ever when I reached Allen. For there, indeed, I found the hill deserted and lonely, and my father's palace all in ruins and overgrown with grass and weeds.

I turned slowly away, and afterwards fared through the land in every direction in search of my friends. But I met only crowds of little people, all strangers, who gazed at me with wonder, and none knew me. I visited every place throughout the country where I knew the Fena had lived, but I found their houses all like Allen, solitary and in ruins and overgrown with grass and weeds.

At length I came to Glenasmole, where many a time I had hunted in days of old with the Fena, and there I saw a crowd of people in the glen.

As soon as they saw me, one of them came forward and said: "Come to us, thou mighty hero, and help us out of our strait, for thou art a man of vast strength."

I went to them, and found a number of men trying in vain to raise a large, flat stone. It was half-lifted from the ground, but those who were under it were not strong enough either to raise it further or to free themselves from its weight. And they were in great distress, and on the point of being crushed to death.

I thought it a shameful thing that so many men should be unable to lift this stone, which Oscar, if he were alive, would take in his right hand and fling over the heads of the feeble crowd. After I had looked a little while, I stooped forward and seized the flag with one hand; and, putting forth my strength, I flung it seven perches from its place, and relieved the little men. But with the great strain the golden saddle-girth broke, and, bounding forward to keep myself from falling, I suddenly came to the ground on my two feet.

The moment the white steed felt himself free, he shook himself and neighed. Then, starting off with the speed of a cloud-shadow on a March day, he left me standing helpless and sorrowful. Instantly a woeful change came over me: the sight of my eyes began to fade, the ruddy beauty of my face fled, I lost all my strength, and I fell to the earth, a poor, withered old man, blind and wrinkled and feeble.

The white steed was never seen again. I never recovered my sight, my youth, or my strength; and I have lived in this manner, sorrowing without ceasing for my gentle, golden-haired wife, Niamh, and thinking ever of my father, Finn, and of the lost companions of my youth.

St. Brigid's Cloak

BY PATRICK KENNEDY

he King of Leinster at that time was not particularly generous, and St. Brigid found it not easy to make him contribute in a respectable fashion to her many charities. One day when he proved more than usually niggardly, she at last said, as it were in jest: "Well, at least grant me as much land as I can cover with my cloak." And, to get rid of her importunity, he consented.

They were at the time standing on the highest point of ground of the Curragh, and she directed four of her sisters to spread out the cloak preparatory to her taking possession. They accordingly took up the garment, but instead of laying it flat on the turf, each virgin, with face turned to a different point of the compass, began to run swiftly, the cloth expanding at their wish in all directions. Other pious ladies, as the border enlarged, seized portions of it to preserve something of a circular shape, and the elastic extension continued till the breadth was a mile at least.

"Oh, St. Brigid," said the frighted King, "what are you about?"

"I am—or rather my cloak is—about to cover your whole province to punish you for your stinginess to the poor."

"Oh! Come! Come! This won't do. Call your maidens back. I will give you a decent plot of ground, and be more liberal for the future."

The saint was easily persuaded, She obtained some acres, and if the King held his purse-strings tight on any future occasion she had only to allude to her cloak's miraculous qualities to bring him to reason.

The Giant's Stairs

BY T. CROFTON CROKER

O n the road between Passage and Cork there is an old mansion called Ronayne's Court. It may be easily known from the stack of chimneys and the gable ends, which are to be seen, look at it which way you will. Here it was that Maurice Ronayne and his wife Margaret Gould kept house, as may be learned to this day from the great old chimney-piece, on which is carved their arms. They were a mighty worthy couple, and had but one son, who was called Philip, after no less a person than the King of Spain.

Immediately on his smelling the cold air of this world the child sneezed, which was naturally taken to be a good sign of his having a clear head; and the subsequent rapidity of his learning was truly amazing, for on the very first day a primer was put into his hands he tore out the A, B, C page and destroyed it as a thing quite beneath his notice. No wonder then that both father and mother were proud of their heir, who gave such indisputable proofs of genius, or, as they called it in that part of the world, "genus".

One morning, however, Master Phil, who was then just seven years old, was missing, and no one could tell what had become of him. Servants were sent in all directions to seek him, on horse-back and on foot, but they returned without any tidings of the boy, whose disappearance altogether was most unaccountable. A large reward was offered, but it produced them no intelligence, and years rolled away without Mr. and Mrs. Ronayne having obtained any satisfactory account of the fate of their lost child.

There lived at this time, near Carrigaline, one Robin Kelly, a blacksmith by trade. He was what is termed a handyman, and his abilities were held in much estimation by the lads and the lasses of the neighbourhood. For, independent of shoeing horses, which he did to great perfection, and making plough-irons, he interpreted dreams for the young women, sung "Arthur O'Bradley" at their weddings, and was so good-natured a fellow at a christening, that he was gossip to half the country round.

Now it happened that Robin had a dream himself, and young Philip Ronayne appeared to him in it, at the dead hour of the night. Robin thought he saw the boy mounted upon a beautiful white horse, and that he told him how he was made a page to the giant Mahon Mac Mahon, who had carried him off, and who held his Court in the hard heart of the rock.

"The seven years—my time of service—are clean out, Robin," said he. "If you release me this night I will be the making of you for ever after."

"And how will I know," said Robin—cunning enough, even in his sleep—"but this is all a dream?"

"Take that," said the boy, "for a token." And at the word the white horse struck out with one of his hind legs, and gave poor Robin such a kick in the forehead that, thinking he was a dead man, he roared as loud as he could after his brains, and woke up calling a thousand murders. He found himself in bed, but he had the mark of the blow, the regular print of a horse-shoe upon his forehead as red as blood. Robin Kelly, who never before found himself puzzled at the dream of any other person, did not know what to think of his own.

Robin was well acquainted with the Giant's Stairs—as, indeed, who is not who knows the harbour? They consist of great masses of rock, which, piled one above another, rise like a flight of steps from very deep water, against the bold cliff of Carrigmahon. Nor are they badly suited for stairs to those who have legs of sufficient length to stride over a moderate-sized house, or to enable them to clear the space of a mile in a hop, step, and jump. Both these feats the giant Mac Mahon was said to have performed in the days of Finnian glory, and the common tradition of the country placed his dwelling within the cliff up whose side the stairs led.

Such was the impression which the dream made on Robin, that he determined to put its truth to the test. It occurred to him, however, before setting out on this adventure, that a plough-iron may be no bad companion, as, from experience, he knew it was an excellent knockdown argument, having on more occasions than one settled a little disagreement very quietly. So, putting one on his shoulder, off he marched in the cool of the evening, through Glaun a Thowk (The Hawk's Glen) to Monkstown.

Here an old gossip of his (Tom Clancey by name) lived, who, on hearing Robin's dream, promised him the use of his skiff, and moreover offered to assist in rowing it to the Giant's Stairs.

After a supper which was of the best, they embarked. It was a beautiful still night, and the little boat glided swiftly along. The regular dip of the oars, the distant song of the sailor, and sometimes the voice of a belated traveller at the ferry of Carrigaloe, alone broke the quietness of the land and sea and sky. The tide was in their favour, and in a few minutes Robin and his gossip rested on their oars under the shadow of the Giant's Stairs.

Robin looked anxiously for the entrance to the Giant's palace, which, it was said, may be found by anyone seeking it at midnight, but no such entrance could he see. His impatience had hurried him there before that time, and after waiting a considerable space in a state of suspense not to be described, Robin, with pure vexation, could not help exclaiming to his companion: " 'Tis a pair of fools we are, Tom Clancey, for coming here at all on the strength of a dream!"

"And whose doing is it," said Tom, "but your own?"

At that moment they perceived a faint glimmering of light to proceed from the cliff, which gradually increased until a porch big enough for a king's palace unfolded itself almost on a level with the water. They pulled the skiff directly towards the opening, and Robin Kelly, seizing his plough-iron, boldly entered with a strong hand and a stout heart.

Wild and strange was that entrance. The whole of it appeared formed of grim and grotesque faces, blending so strangely each with the other that it was impossible to define any. The chin of one formed the nose of another; what appeared to be a fixed and stern eye, if dwelt upon, changed to a gaping mouth; and the lines of the lofty forehead grew into a majestic and flowing beard. The more Robin allowed himself to contemplate the forms around him, the more terrifying they became, and the stony expressions of this crook of faces assumed a savage ferocity as his imagination converted feature after feature into a different shape and character.

Losing the twilight in which these indefinite forms were visible, he advanced through a dark and devious passage, whilst a deep and rumbling noise sounded as if the rock was about to close upon him and swallow him up alive for ever. Now, indeed, poor Robin felt afraid. "Robin, Robin," said he, "if you were a fool for coming here, what in the name of fortune are you now?"

But, as before, he had scarcely spoken, when he saw a small light twinkling through the darkness of the distance, like a star in the midnight sky. To retreat was out of the question because so many turnings and windings were in the passage, that he considered he had but little chance of making his way back. He therefore proceeded towards the bit of light, and came at last into a spacious chamber, from the roof of which hung the solitary lamp that had guided him. Emerging from such profound gloom, the single lamp afforded Robin abundant light to discover several gigantic figures seated round a massive stone table, as if in serious deliberation, but no word disturbed the breathless silence which prevailed.

At the head of this table sat Mahon Mac Mahon himself, whose majestic beard had taken root, and in the course of ages grown into the stone slab. He was the first who perceived Robin, and, instantly starting up, drew his long beard from out the huge piece of rock in such haste and with so sudden a jerk that it was shattered into a thousand pieces.

"What seek you?" he demanded in a voice of thunder.

"I come," answered Robin, with as much boldness as he could put on, for his heart was almost fainting within him, "I come," said he, "to claim Philip Ronayne, whose time of service is out this night."

"And who sent you here?" said the giant.

" 'Twas of my own accord I came," said Robin.

"Then you must single him out from among my pages," said the giant, "and if you fix on the wrong one, you life is forfeit. Follow me."

He led Robin into a hall of vast extent, and filled with lights, along either side of which were rows of beautiful children, all apparently seven years old, and none beyond that age, dressed in green, and every one exactly dressed alike.

"Here," said Mahon, "you are free to take Philip Ronayne, if you will. But remember, I give but one choice."

Robin was sadly perplexed, for there were hundreds of children and he had no very clear recollection of the boy he sought. But he walked along the hall, by the side of Mahon, as if nothing was the matter, although his great iron dress clanked fearfully at every step, sounding louder than Robin's own sledge battering on his anvil.

They had nearly reached the end without speaking, when Robin, seeing that the only means he had was to make friends with the giant, determined to try what effect a few soft words might have.

" 'Tis a fine wholesome appearance the poor children carry," remarked Robin, "although they have been here so long shut out from the fresh air and the blessed light of heaven. 'Tis tenderly your honour must have reared them."

"Ay," said the giant, "that is true for you. So give me your hand—for you are, I believe, a very honest fellow for a black-smith."

Robin at the first look did not much like the huge size of the hand, and therefore presented his plough-iron which, the giant seizing, twisted in his grasp round and round again as if it had been a potato stalk; on seeing this all the children set up a shout of laughter.

In the midst of their mirth Robin thought he heard his name called. All ear and eye, he put his hand on the boy who he fancied had spoken, crying out at the same time: "Let me live or die for it, but this is young Phil Ronayne."

"It is Philip Ronayne—happy Philip Ronayne," said his young companions; and in an instant the hall became dark. Crashing noises were heard, and all was in strange confusion, but Robin held fast his prize, and found himself lying in the grey dawn of the morning at the head of the Giant's Stairs with the boy clasped in his arms.

Robin had plenty of gossips to spread the story of his wonderful adventure. Passage, Monkstown, Carrigaline—the whole barony of Kerricurrihy rung with it.

"Are you quite sure, Robin, it is young Phil Ronayne you have brought back with you?" was the regular question; for although the boy had been seven years away, his appearance now was just the same as on the day he was missed. He had neither grown taller nor older in look, and he spoke of things which had happened before he was carried off as one awakened from sleep, or as if they had occurred yesterday.

"Am I sure? Well, that's a queer question," was Robin's reply. "Seeing the boy has the blue eyes of his mother, with the foxy hair of the father, to say nothing of the purty wart on the right side of his little nose."

However Robin Kelly may have been questioned, the worthy couple of Ronayne's Court doubted not that he was the deliverer of their child from the power of the giant Mac Mahon; and the reward they bestowed on him equalled their gratitude.

Philip Ronayne lived to be an old man; and he was remarkable to the day of his death for his skill in working brass and iron, which it was believed he had learned during his seven years' apprenticeship to the giant Mahon Mac Mahon.

The Crookened Back

BY T. CROFTON CROKER

Peggy Barrett was once tall, well-shaped and comely. She was in her youth remarkable for two qualities, not often found together, of being the most thrifty housewife, and the best dancer in her native village of Ballyhooley.

But she is now upwards of sixty years old, and during the last ten years of her life she has never been able to stand upright. Her back is bent nearly to a level, yet she has the freest use of all her limbs that can be enjoyed in such a posture. Her health is good and her mind vigorous, and, in the family of her eldest son, with whom she has lived since the death of her husband, she performs all the domestic services which her age, and the infirmity just mentioned, allow. She washes the potatoes, makes the fire, sweeps the house (labours in which she good-humouredly says she finds her crooked back mighty convenient), plays with the children, and tells stories to the family and their neighbouring friends, who often collect round her son's fireside to hear them during the long winter evenings.

Her powers of conversation are highly extolled, both for humour and narration, and anecdotes of droll or awkward incidents, connected with the posture in which she has been so long fixed as well as the history of the occurrence to which she owes that misfortune, are favourite topics of her discourse. Among other matters she is fond of relating how, on a certain day, at the close of a bad harvest, when several tenants of the estate on which she lived concerted in a field a petition for an abatement of rent, they placed the paper on which they wrote upon her back, which was found no very inconvenient substitute for a table.

Peggy, like all experienced story-tellers, suited her tales, both in length and subject, to the audience and the occasion. She knew that, in broad daylight, when the sun shines brightly, and the

107

trees are budding, and the birds singing around us, when men and women like ourselves are moving and speaking, employed variously in business or amusement, when we are engaged about the realities of life and nature, we want that spirit of credulity without which tales of the deepest interest will lose their power. At such times Peggy was brief, very particular as to facts, and never dealt in the marvellous.

But round the blazing hearth of a Christmas evening, when infidelity is banished from all companies, at least in low and simple life, as a quality, to say the least of it, out of season; when the winds of "dark December" whistled bleakly round the walls, and almost through the doors of the little mansion, reminding its inmates that as the world is vexed by elements superior to human power, so it may be visited by beings of a superior nature. At such times would Peggy Barrett give full scope to her memory, or her imagination, or both, and upon one of these occasions she gave the following circumstantial account of the "crookening of her back".

"It was, of all days in the year, the day before May-day, that I went out to the garden to weed the potatoes. I would not have gone out that day but I was dull in myself, and sorrowful, and wanted to be alone. All the boys and girls were laughing and joking in the house, making goaling-balls and dressing out ribbons for the mummers next day. I couldn't bear it.

" 'Twas only at the Easter that was then past (and that's ten years last Easter—I won't forget the time), that I buried my poor man. I thought how gay and joyful I was, many a long year before that, at the May-eve before our wedding, when with Robin by my side I sat cutting and sewing the ribbons for the goaling-ball I was to give the boys on the next day, proud to be preferred above all the other girls of the banks of the Blackwater by the handsomest boy and the best hurler in the village.

"So I left the house and went to the garden. I stayed there all day, and didn't come home to dinner. I don't know how it was but somehow I continued on, weeding and thinking sorrowfully enough, and singing over some of the old songs that I sung many and many a time in the days that are gone, and for them that never will come back to me to hear them. The truth is, I hated to go and sit silent and mournful among the people in the house, that were merry and young, and had the best of their days before them.

" 'Twas late before I thought of returning home, and I did not leave the garden till some time after sunset. The moon was up, but though there wasn't a cloud to be seen, and though a star was winking here and there in the sky, the day wasn't long enough gone to have it clear moonlight. Still it shone enough to make everything on one side of the heavens look pale and silvery-like, and the thin white mist was just beginning to creep along the fields. On the other side, near where the sun was set, there was more of day-light, and the sky looked angry, red, and fiery through the trees, like as if it was lighted up by a great town burning below. Everything was as silent as a churchyard, only now and then one could hear far off a dog barking, or a cow lowing after being milked. There wasn't a creature to be seen on the road or in the fields.

"I wondered at this first, but then I remembered it was May-eve, and that many a thing, both good and bad, would be wandering about that night, and that I ought to shun danger as well as others. So I walked on as quick as I could, and soon came to the end of the demesne wall, where the trees rise high and thick at each side of the road, and almost meet at the top. My heart misgave me when I got under the shade. There was so much light let down from the opening above that I could see about a stone-throw before me.

"All of a sudden I heard a rustling among the branches, on the right side of the road, and saw something like a small black goat, only with long wide horns turned out instead of being bent backwards, standing upon its hind legs upon the top of the wall, and looking down on me. My breath was stopped, and I couldn't move for near a minute. I couldn't help, somehow, keeping my eyes fixed on it, and it never stirred but kept looking in the same fixed way down at me.

"I made a rush, and went on; but I didn't go ten steps when I saw the very same sight on the wall, to the left of me, standing in exactly the same manner, but three or four times as high, and almost as tall as the tallest man. The horns looked frightful. It gazed upon me as before; my legs shook, my teeth chattered, and I thought I would drop down dead every moment.

"At last I felt as if I was obliged to go on, and on I went, but it was without feeling how I moved, or whether my legs carried me. Just as I passed the spot where this frightful thing was standing, I heard a noise as if something sprung from the wall, and felt as if a heavy animal plumped down upon me, and held with the fore-feet clinging to my shoulders, and the hind ones fixed in my gown, that was folded and pinned up behind me. 'Tis

the wonder of my life ever since how I bore the shock, but so it was.

"I neither fell, nor even staggered with the weight, but walked on as if I had the strength of ten men, though I felt as if I couldn't help moving, and couldn't stand still if I wished it. Though I gasped with fear, I knew as well as I do now what I was doing. I tried to cry out, but couldn't. I tried to run, but wasn't able. I tried to look back, but my head and neck were as if they were screwed in a vice. I could barely roll my eyes on each side, and then I could see, as clearly and plainly as if it was in the broad light of the blessed sun, a black and cloven foot planted upon each of my shoulders. I heard a low breathing in my ear. I felt, at every step I took, my leg strike back against the feet of the creature that was on my back. Still I could do nothing but walk straight on.

"Now I came within sight of the house, and a welcome sight it was to me, for I thought I would be released when I reached it. I soon came close to the door, but it was shut to, for they were more cautious about May-eve than I was. I saw the light inside, through the chinks of the door. I heard 'em talking and laughing within. I felt myself at three yards' distance from them that would die to save me. May the Lord save me from ever again feeling what I did that night, when I found myself held by what couldn't be good nor friendly, but without the power to help myself, or to call my friends, or to put out my hand to knock, or even to lift my leg to strike the door, and let them know that I was outside. 'Twas as if my hands grew to my sides, and my feet were glued to the ground, or had the weight of a rock fixed to them.

"Then I thought of blessing myself, and my right hand, that would do nothing else, did that for me. Still the weight remained on my back, and all was as before. I blessed myself again: 'twas still all the same. I then gave myself up for lost: but I blessed myself a third time, and my hand no sooner finished the sign, than all at once I felt the burthen spring off of my back. The door flew open as if a clap of thunder burst it, and I was pitched forward on my forehead in upon the middle of the floor. When I got up my back was crookened, and I never stood straight from that night to this blessed hour."

There was a pause when Peggy Barrett finished. Those who had heard the story before had listened with a look of half-satisfied interest, blended, however, with an expression of that serious and solemn feeling which always attends a tale of supernatural wonders, how ever often told. They moved upon their seats out of the posture in which they had remained fixed during the narrative, and sat in an attitude which denoted that their curiosity as to the cause of this strange occurrence had been long since allayed. Those to whom it was before unknown still retained their look and posture of strained attention, and anxious but solemn expectation.

A grandson of Peggy's, about nine years old (not the child of the son with whom she lived), had never before heard the story. As it grew in interest, he was observed to cling closer and closer to the old woman's side, and at the close he was gazing steadfastly at her, with his body bent back across her knees, and his face turned up to hers, with a look through which a disposition to weep seemed contending with curiosity. After a moment's pause he could no longer restrain his impatience, and catching her grey locks in one hand, while the tear of dread and wonder was just dropping from his eyelash, he cried: "Granny, what was it?"

The old woman smiled first at the elder part of her audience, and then at her grandson, and patting him on the forehead, she said: "It was the Pooka."